DICTIONARY OF
SUPERSTITIONS

DICTIONARY OF
SUPERSTITIONS

Cécile Donner
and Jean-Luc Caradeau

Translated by Richard LeFanu

GRANADA
London Toronto Sydney New York

Granada Publishing Limited
8 Grafton Street, London W1X 3LA

Published by Granada Publishing 1985

Copyright © International Book Promotion, 1984, Paris

British Library Cataloguing in Publication Data

Caradeau, Jean-Luc
  Dictionary of superstitions.
  1. Superstition—Dictionaries
  I. Title   II. Donner, Cécile
  398'.41   BF1025

ISBN 0 246 12861 5
     0 246 12420 2 (Pbk)

Printed in Great Britain by Mackays of Chatham Limited

This edition has been adapted for the British market by
Jennifer Westwood.

CONTENTS

INTRODUCTION

Throughout the world, popular wisdom attributes the hand of fate to countless acts and events; some of these signs are favourable, others malign.

The omens are everywhere; they permeate our daily lives. Do you know, for example, that the way you sweep up may be fraught with consequences? If wrongly used, the broom sweeps luck away. A broken mirror guarantees seven years' bad luck; did you know it is possible to exorcize this evil omen? It's true that a horseshoe brings good luck, but only if you know the right way to put it up. It's possible to summon up money and we will show you how. Do you wish to protect yourself or to conjure up good luck? A small piece of coal in your pocket or your handbag will do the trick. Do you want to know how to keep the affections of your loved one? This book will provide the answer.

It is essential to know how to recognize and interpret these signs, so as to be able to make good use of some of them and to protect yourself from others. This *Dictionary of Superstitions* gives you a detailed and complete list of every one of them, classified alphabetically. It also tells you about the gestures and rites you should perform in order to break evil spells and attract good luck.

In this book, everyone can discover how to become master of his or her fate.

Avidly curious since his earliest years, Jean-Luc Caradeau has practised hypnosis from the age of sixteen. He later became interested in testing the effectiveness of parapsychological and magical techniques, and with a number of friends set up a traditional research group in which he carried out numerous experiments and worked with several Psi subjects. It was during this period that he discovered the treasures hidden in popular traditions all over the world.

In 1975 he became a free-lance journalist specializing in the esoteric tradition. He has written hundreds of articles about magical practices throughout the world and about cosmology, esoteric lore and parapsychology. Besides his literary activities, he practises hypnotism, parapsychology and magic.

On 1 June 1982, he produced a programme on 'France-Inter' with the famous clairvoyante Marie Delclos, which was the first successful experiment in telepathy in a radio broadcast. As a member of several 'traditional' societies of various schools of thought, he is recognized as one of the leading practitioners of Sacred Magic.

Jean-Luc Caradeau is today one of those rare scholars who can link these popular secrets to the most hermetic magical and religious cosmologies. Wishing to make his knowledge more generally accessible, he now offers this practical handbook as Everyman's 'Bible of Luck'.

Cécile Donner is self-taught. At an early age, she became passionately interested in the esoteric sciences and in the interpretation of the laws which govern them. Her innate feeling for study and research enabled her, in the space of a few years, to become one of the leading specialists in natural and traditional medicine.

As a free-lance journalist, her articles in specialist reviews are greatly appreciated by her readers as well as by practitioners of alternative medicine, who have a great respect for her profound knowledge of the properties of plants and of the magical traditions associated with them.

Her literary work includes numerous articles on traditions throughout the world, on natural medicine, clairvoyance and parapsychology, many of which were written in collaboration with Jean-Luc Caradeau. As a scholar and a writer, Cécile Donner has for several years made it her task to reveal and explain to her readers the secrets of the eternal knowledge which can be found in the traditions of many lands.

AEROPLANE

Aeroplanes: how to ward off accidents

If you're flying

Don't use any word which might conjure up an air disaster, such as 'forced landing', 'crash', 'explosion'.

Flowers are forbidden on the plane

All flowers are forbidden – but the most ill-omened are *white*.

The unluckiest object of all that one can bring on to a plane is a mixed bunch of *white* and *red* flowers (see also **HOSPITAL**).

Our advice

You or one of your fellow-passengers may be unable to avoid incurring one of these bad omens.

Before setting off for the airport, put on one of your **AMULET(S)** and touch **WOOD**. As you step on to the plane:

1. cross your fingers; or
2. make the sign of the cross; or
3. spit.

AGE

Never tell anybody your age

To tell a person your age is extremely unlucky. Like all counting and numbering, it exposes you to risk. Never, under any circumstances, tell anyone your true age.

Our advice

Always alter it by one or two years, or turn it into a round figure, so as not to give away any information which could be used against you.

AMULET

Wear your amulet

An amulet is an object carried on your person, kept in your home or placed among your possessions, which has the power to protect you against such dangers as lightning, shipwreck or the **EVIL EYE**.

Amulets may be

A. *Animal*

> *Examples:* a rabbit's foot
> sharks' teeth

B. *Vegetable*

> *Examples:* **GARLIC**
> **NUTMEG**
> potato

C. *Mineral*

> *Examples:* **COAL**
> 'cold iron' (e.g. **AXE**, **HORSESHOE**)
> horsebrasses

Manufactured amulets

You may buy ready-made amulets or make them yourself. They are no less powerful than the natural kind, especially when you have carried them for some time and they are imbued with your life-essence.

> *Examples:* open hand with fingers stretched
> a hand making horns
> a hand making the 'fig'

the 'Eye of Horus'
the 'Hand of Fatima'

1. *A hand making a horn*   **2.** *A hand making a 'fig'*

Amuletic jewellery

Some jewellery has amuletic properties and will ward off diseases and the Evil Eye.

Wear: blue beads – against the Evil Eye
a copper bracelet – against arthritis
a coral necklace – against malign influences
gold earrings – (for seamen) against drowning

Note Only plain gold 'sleepers' are good for this purpose – screw-on earrings have no power.

Written amulets

These can be secret signs, spells, charms or verses from the Bible written on a slip of paper or parchment, and hung in a small bag round your neck.

Important

The main function of an amulet is to *protect* you. For luck-bringing charms, see under **TALISMAN**.

How to use your amulets

Wear them: round your neck, on a bracelet or watch-chain. For animals: hang them round their necks or attach them to their collars.

3

Carry them: in your pocket, briefcase or handbag.
Bind them: on your tools, implements, weapons.
Nail them: to your house, cattleshed, storehouse.
Tie them: to a tree in a garden or near a field with growing crops, and to dangerous places such as a **BRIDGE**.

AXE

Axe: good or bad?

Like other sharp-edged implements made of iron or steel, an axe can be either lucky or unlucky, depending on the circumstances.

Dreaming about an axe

To dream of an axe is unlucky: it is an omen of death or at least terrible danger.

Carrying an axe through the house

To carry an axe *on your shoulder* through the house is very unlucky. It will bring disaster on the occupants (cf. **SPADE**).

Our advice

Put it under your arm.

BABY

Ensure a baby's luck right from the start

His first gift

As his very first gift, you should give a baby a silver sixpence, if you have one; if not, any other small silver coin.

Watch what he does

The sixpence should be placed in his right hand: if he grasps it tightly, he will be careful with his money, if he drops it, a spendthrift.

His first visit

You will further increase the child's potential for good luck by giving him an egg, bread, salt and a box of matches: the food to ensure that he never comes to want, the salt and the matches (=fire) to protect him against evil.

These gifts may be given to the new-born child when you first visit him, but better still when he first comes to your house.

His christening gift

If you are a godparent or grandparent, or someone else close to the child, try to give him as his christening gift the sort of old-fashioned teething-ring known as a 'coral-and-bells'. The red coral will be his **AMULET** against the **EVIL EYE**, the bells will ward off evil spirits, especially if they are silver ones.

Ensure the luck of your own baby

Wrap him in something old: only after this has been done should he wear the new garments that have been made for him.

Carry him upstairs before you carry him down: if his first journey is upwards, he will rise in life.

Our advice

If you live in an apartment or a house with only one floor, make the baby's first journey by stepping up on to a box or stool while you are carrying him. This will fulfil the condition and ensure his luck.

BASEBALL

Baseball: observe the rules

Take care before the game

- If a player should bump into a clergyman, he can stave off bad luck if he keeps his fingers crossed (middle finger over forefinger) until he sees a dog outside the stadium.
- A player who sees a cross-eyed *man* in the crowd will have good luck, but if it is a *woman*, he will make no runs, unless he spits through his fingers without letting her see him do it.
- A hair-pin given by a red-haired woman in the crowd (her hair must be natural, not dyed) is a powerful **TALISMAN** for a player. He will play like a demon.

Keep your eyes open during training

A bat falling in front of a player foretells an injury in the next game.

A bat falling in front of the team manager foretells a season of defeats.

A broken bat means bad luck for the whole team.

A special case

A dog crossing the field before the game brings bad luck to the players and increases the risk of accidents. There's no way of averting this omen.

Our advice

To help ward off ill omens, follow these simple rules:

1. When you buy a new bat, spit on it crosswise. This will bring you luck.
2. Never lend your bat. It contains a limited number of winning hits. In lending it, you give a certain number of them to the borrower.
3. In the changing-room, make sure your mitt has the fingers pointing downwards.
4. Before putting on your mitt, spit on your hands and rub them together.

5. Before pitching, 'blow cold' on the ball (i.e. blow with the lips together).

BEANS

Broad beans: the smell of their blossom is unlucky

Never sleep where you can smell the blossom of broad beans: it may give you nightmares and evil visions.

But beans themselves are lucky

They will drive away evil spirits and bring good fortune.

Our advice

Celebrate New Year's Eve as the Japanese do. The head of your household must put on his or her best clothes, then walk through every room of the house at midnight, scattering roasted beans and saying 'Out, demons! In, luck!'

BED

Don't place your bed so that it points north and south

You spend a third of your life in your bed. Avoid putting it in a position which brings evil influences to bear on you.

You should not:

- position your bed so that it points north and south;
- stand it at an angle to floorboards or exposed beams;
- set it across the corner of a room.

These three strictures are set out in ascending order of import-

7

ance, the second being more important than the first and the third more important than the second.

You should:

- stand your bed so that it points east and west;
- place it so that it points in the same direction as floorboards and exposed beams;
- place it parallel to a wall.

Direction to be avoided

N

W

E

Most favourable direction

Most favourable direction

S

Direction to be avoided

To increase your luck

Don't turn your mattress on a Sunday or Friday.

Don't get out of bed in the morning on the same side as you got into it the previous night. A person who has 'got out of bed on the wrong side' may be bad-tempered all day.

Don't put an umbrella on a bed: this is very unlucky.

BEE

The bee: a messenger of luck

If a bee comes into your house, it is a sign of good luck or of a stranger coming to visit.

The omen of the bee is obviously more significant in big cities than in the country (where bees are more numerous).

Warning! The bee must be allowed to enter and leave of its own accord. If it is caught or driven out, this is very unlucky.

Never kill a bee. Such an act could bring you several years' bad luck.

Our advice

Even if the visit heralded by the bee seems insignificant at the time, you should attach great importance to it. What seems insignificant today may be of cardinal importance tomorrow. Even if no visitor is involved, pay close attention to the behaviour of the bee: if a honey-bee alights on one's hand, it is a sign of money to come, if it settles on one's head, a sign of future fame.

A note to bee-keepers

If you keep bees, remember that *it is unlucky to buy or sell them.* Bought bees will not prosper.

Our advice

Particularly when starting bee-keeping, try to borrow a swarm, on the understanding that you will repay it if the giver ever loses his bees.

Telling the bees

To maintain their luck, bee-keepers must always *tell their bees* everything that goes on in the family: births, marriages and deaths, and any other notable events. Otherwise they may lose their bees and their good fortune.

BIBLE

The Bible can bring luck to every home

The Bible can be used in many ways as a protection for your home.

Our advice

- Place an open Bible in your baby's cot to keep it from harm.
- Lay one under the pillow at night to protect the sleeper: this will also help children learn to read.
- Put a leaf from a Bible under your doorstep, where it will cause a thief to stumble and wake the house.

Foretelling the future using a Bible

To find out if the coming year will be lucky for you or unlucky, open a Bible at random on New Year's morning and, without looking at the page, lay your finger on it. The verse you have thus chosen will forecast the nature of events to come. You may use the same method to seek advice in any difficulty.

Note You must do this fasting.

BLACK CAT

A black cat: lucky or unlucky?

To meet a black cat brings good luck or bad luck depending on where you live. In the United States of America and some countries of Europe, a white cat is lucky, a black one unlucky. In Britain the opposite is true.

- To meet a black cat is generally a *good* omen, especially if it crosses your path.
- The omen may be *bad* if the cat crosses your path from left to right, or turns back or runs away from you.

Our advice

Try not to frighten the cat away, but ensure your good luck by stroking it three times and greeting it politely.

In the house

All this, of course, applies to cats met outside the house. Households actually owning a black cat are very fortunate.

If a strange black cat enters your house, especially if it comes uninvited, it is a very good sign. Do not chase it away or it will take the luck of the house with it.

This applies only to cats which are *completely* black.

A special case

To have a black cat on board a ship, especially if it comes of its own accord, is extremely lucky.

The fisherman's wife who keeps a black cat in the house will ensure that her husband always comes safely home from sea.

BREAD

Bread: handle with care

Take heed!

- Putting a loaf upside down on the table brings bad luck – even if this is done accidentally.
- Bread must never be burned or thrown away: the person who does so will live to go hungry.
- Bread must not be cut at both ends, or taken hold of by one person when another person is cutting it.
- It is unlucky to take the last slice of bread and butter off a plate unless it is offered to you. But if it *is* offered, never refuse it, for it will bring you luck in love and money.

When you are baking

- Make a cross on the dough when setting it to rise: this will protect it from the influence of the Devil.
- Only one person must put the bread in the oven: if two people do it, they will quarrel.
- While it is baking, no other loaf in the house should be cut with a knife, or the new batch will spoil. If you need bread during that time, it must be broken.

Our advice

If you bake bread on Christmas Day or Good Friday, keep a loaf in the house for the year to come, and it will protect it from fire and its inhabitants from misfortune.

Bread baked on Good Friday will never go mouldy. Crumbs grated from a loaf that has become dry and hard, if mixed in hot water, will speedily cure diarrhoea.

BRIDGE

A bridge can be ill-omened

Take great care

Don't be the first person to cross over a new bridge.

Don't talk when standing or walking under a bridge.

Don't pass under a railway bridge while a train is running overhead, or stand on the road over a railway while a train is passing below.

Don't part from somebody on or under a bridge: if you do so, it's certain you'll never see them again.

BROOM

The broom: if not properly used, it can sweep luck away

How to protect yourself

Here are strict rules which you must observe:

1. Never sweep the dust straight out of the door, or you will sweep out your good fortune with it. This is particularly to be avoided by a bride sweeping her new home for the first time.
2. Always sweep inwards, into the middle of the room, and gather up the dust with a dustpan. Then you may carry it outside.

3. Always clean the upstairs rooms before noon: if you carry dust down the stairs after that, a corpse will soon follow.

Days and seasons to avoid

Don't sweep your house at all on New Year's Day or on Good Friday; it will cause the death of someone in the family.

Don't sweep your house with an old-fashioned besom of birch or broom during May:

> If you sweep the house with broom in May,
> You'll sweep the head of the house away.

Don't buy (or make) a broom in the month of May or during the Twelve Days of Christmas.

Don't sweep a room in which a guest has been staying until he or she has been gone some hours: to do the work too soon will prevent him from ever returning.

BUTTON

Take care to button your clothes properly

Doing up a button in the wrong hole

If you do up a button in the wrong hole, you must unbutton the garment, take it right off and start again, buttoning it correctly.

Note Hooks are subject to exactly the same rule.

Always do up an odd number of buttons

- If your garment has only *one button*, you can safely do it up or leave it open.
- If it has *two buttons*, only do up the top one, or wear it open.
- If it has *three buttons*, do up all three or only the middle one: never do up two.

Our advice

Always do up the *inside* button of a dress, a suit or a double-breasted jacket.

13

CAMEO

The cameo brings happiness

Grandmother's talisman

Cameos are pieces of jewellery which are often passed on from generation to generation in one family. If you possess a cameo, wear it every day as your personal **TALISMAN**. It will continue to bring good luck to your child if you leave it to him or her, and will help one member of the family in each generation.

Buying a cameo

If you buy a cameo, cherish it for seven years, and at the end of that time it will become your talisman.

Our advice

Ladies: thread the cameo on a black velvet ribbon and wear it round your neck. In this way you will be able to wear it both by day and by night.

Men: have the cameo made into a tie-pin. This is both unostentatious and elegant, and you will be able to wear it every day.

CANDLE

The light of a candle tells you your fate

Revelations you can read in the candle-flame

- If the flame burns blue, there will be a death in the family.
- If the flame gutters and sways, although there is no draught, windy weather is coming.
- If the wick refuses to light, there will be rain.

14

The way the wax runs can foretell death

If the streams of wax running down the candle spread out into folds, forming a 'winding-sheet', it is an omen of death for the person sitting opposite or someone else in the family.

If there is a spark in the wick

A spark in the wick foretells the arrival of strangers, or else a letter for the person nearest it.

If you snuff a candle accidentally

This is a sign of a wedding.

Respect the candle

Don't light a candle from a burning flame, but kindle a new flame with a lighter or better still a match. To light a candle from the fire in the **HEARTH** is particularly unlucky: the person who does so will certainly die poor.

Don't let a candle gutter out. Blow it out or snuff it out with your fingers, otherwise misfortune will come to someone in the house.

Don't leave a candle burning in an empty room: this is very ill-omened. If it is left for any length of time, a death will certainly follow.

Exception This is the *Christmas candle*, which should be left burning all through the night of Christmas Eve to ensure prosperity in the coming year. It should be lit by the head of the household or oldest member of the family, and blown or snuffed out by him in the morning. It is unlucky to touch it after it has been lit, and if it goes out accidentally, this is a bad omen.

Beware – of three

Never light three candles with a single match.
Never have three candles burning together in the same room.

Our advice

If someone has lit three candles, avert the omen at once by extinguishing one of them, or misfortune will follow.

CAR

Your car can be lucky too

Like any vehicle your car is particularly susceptible to good and bad luck.

Before you go off for a drive or for a long journey, don't on any account tempt fate by telling everyone about your last accident or by boasting about how fast you drive.

When you have a flat tyre (remember not to drive without a spare wheel), get it mended as soon as possible. It's nearly always when you have no spare wheel that you get a flat tyre on the motorway or in the middle of nowhere.

Never have *all* the dents in your bodywork repaired. A vehicle without the smallest scratch or bump attracts dents irresistibly. But a small and barely visible dent will save you from countless accidents.

When you change cars

If you have hung a little mascot in the vehicle you are going to sell or stuck stickers on the windows, you should avoid making certain mistakes.

A. If the car has been a loyal and trusted servant, without too many accidents or repairs, and you have *happy memories* of the time during which you used it, remove the mascots, stickers and oddments you have installed and put them in your new car: they will protect it and bring it luck (see **AMULET** and **TALISMAN**).

B. If you have *disagreeable memories* of this car, a chapter of inexplicable breakdowns, or the premature wearing out of parts and accessories – in a word, if you are certain you won't miss it – take out all the oddments, but *don't* put them in your new car: they would pass on the bad luck they had accumulated in the old one. The best thing to do is to burn them. There's no need to destroy them completely – contact with a candle flame is enough (and this can be done anywhere).

Our advice

You may think that it is easier to leave these things in your old car: in this way, they would become the property of the new owner and you would be safe. But NO. You would be indissolubly bound by these oddments to the bad luck which attaches to your old car and you would run the risk of becoming yourself the albatross of the new one.

CAT

The cat: a true friend but easily upset

The cat is endowed with psychic powers. It is influenced by Man and in turn influences his fate. You can be sure that a cat who loves you and feels loved will bring you good luck. On the other hand, an unhappy cat is the most certain carrier of bad luck.

How to buy a cat

If you have decided to acquire a cat, you should be guided, not by your personal preferences, but by the unerring finger of fate.

If you are standing by a litter of kittens, go a little nearer and talk to them; one of them will certainly come towards you, while the others take no notice or hide at the back of their cage.

Our advice

Fate is giving you a sign. Don't hesitate: adopt the kitten which comes to you.

The cat protects you

In every house and on every piece of ground there are unlucky places, and your cat will enable you to discover them. If the place where she likes to sit is uncomfortable compared with your cushion or your bed, you can be sure that this part of your house is ill-omened. Don't think of installing your bed or your desk there.

Our advice

Let the cat sit there. The 'malignant waves' which pollute the place do her no harm and, after she has absorbed them, will not affect you either.

The cat: a fortune-teller in the home

Count her sneezes

- If your cat sneezes *once*, rain is coming.
- If she sneezes *three times*, the whole household will get colds.
- If she sneezes *near a bride* on her wedding-morning, no matter how many times, her happiness is assured – her marriage will succeed.

Before going out for a walk, observe your cat

- If she is dashing about or clawing the carpet – *windy weather* is forecast.
- If she is washing over her ears with her paws – it will *rain*.
- If she is sitting with her back to the fire or radiator – there'll be a *frost*.

Be careful

If you are going away, leave your cat in the house or the garden and then listen for a few moments after closing the door. If you hear her crying, this is a very bad omen. It portends some disaster either for you on your journey or for your house during your absence.

Our advice

To avoid this misfortune, go back into the house and find out what your cat wants and see that she is happy. She may be hungry or want a window open, or just want you around. In this last case, if it's at all possible, stay at home.

(See also **BLACK CAT**.)

CAUL

Born with a caul, born to succeed

If your child is born with a caul, he will be lucky and never drown

This good luck will operate in different ways.

18

- If he is a sailor or fisherman, or someone else who travels by sea, he will never suffer shipwreck.
- If he is a lawyer, he will have the gift of eloquence and always win his case.

A special gift

Anyone born with a caul is liable to have Second Sight.

Warning! This luck only operates if the caul has been preserved and is carried by its owner. If it is lost or thrown away, the luck goes with it. If it is sold, for example to a sailor as a charm against drowning, the luck is transferred to him.

So take care of your caul

- Always keep it on your person, wrapped in tissue paper or sewn into a bag.
- Do not part with it – or you will never settle, but be a wanderer all your life.
- Similarly, when you die, arrange for it to be buried or cremated with you, or your spirit will not rest.

CHAIN LETTER

The chain letter: a great swindle

You will doubtless have been the recipient of one of these. The chain letter is in the form of a text, usually extremely badly written, which tells some fantastic story.

Example

The letter claims that the first one in the chain was written by a convict who had escaped from Guatemala or by a leper in Africa. There are many other variations. After this preamble, which is meant to soften you up, there follow directions to copy the text of the letter twenty-five times (or more) and to send it to twenty-five people whom you know. To convince you, it will tell you of two or three people who have won the Pools or made a fortune in record time after obeying this injunction. It then applies the carrot and stick technique and recounts the misfortunes of those who have thrown away this precious document.

Don't be taken in

Nobody – and certainly not the writer of the original letter – could possibly know what became of the missives sent out, even less what happened to those who received them. This letter is therefore a snare and delusion, intended to lure people along a dangerous path. *Take no notice of it – it cannot possibly bring you bad luck.*

CHAIR

Careful with those chairs

Don't knock them over!

It is unlucky to knock a chair over, especially in a hospital. If a nurse happens to do this, she can expect a new patient in the ward.

Don't put your chair back!

If you have been visiting someone's house and a chair has been drawn out for you, don't put it back against the wall as you go. Should you do so, you will never come to that house again.

Our advice

Leave the chair where it is, for its owner to put away.

CHICORY

Chicory: the poor man's mandrake

Oddballs only

If you have an out-of-the-way occupation (e.g. explorer, trapper), wear the *only* **TALISMAN** which will enable you to make exceptional discoveries.

20

The chicory root

For it to become a powerful talisman, it must be pulled out according to an extremely strict ritual.

1. *Choose the day carefully*

A. This root *must* be pulled out between 21 March and 21 September in the northern hemisphere – and between 22 September and 20 March in the southern hemisphere.

B. This operation *must* be carried out on a Saturday between the new moon and the first quarter (in your calendar or your diary: new moon ◉ ; first quarter ☽).

2. *Take the necessary equipment*

Get a bevel-edged plank to use as a spade; a springy branch, tough and fairly long; a piece of kitchen string; and a linen cloth or silk scarf, 30 cm square.

3. *It must be done at a certain hour*

Get to the place where you are going to pull out the chicory on the Friday night, between midnight and 1 am (solar time).

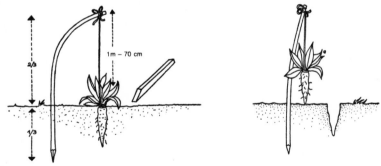

1 m – 70 cm

2/3

1/3

4. *Method*

A. Plant the springy branch in the soil beside the chicory. Take the kitchen string, make a running knot and put it round the chicory.

B. Bend the branch, so as to bring its end down 15 or 20 cm. Tie the free end of the string securely to the end of the branch. The pull exerted by the branch on the string must not be too strong or the running knot will damage the chicory.

C. Using the bevel-edged plank as a spade, loosen the earth round the root. When the root is free, the branch straightens up, lifting the chicory above the soil.

21

D. Put the chicory, which is hanging from the string, on to the cloth or scarf. Bundle up the material, cut the string and go home.

Warning! In the course of these operations, your hands must never touch the chicory – neither the stem nor the root.

5. *Dry your root*

As soon as you get home put the chicory somewhere dark and dry, opening the scarf or the cloth so that the root is exposed to the air. Let the chicory dry, still on its wrapping, for at least six or seven months, turning the root over every three days to prevent it rotting. When it is really dry, the leaves will drop off by themselves and turn to dust. *When the root is dry, put it in your pocket: it is a highly effective talisman.*

Our advice

Never reveal that you have a chicory root in your pocket. If you do so, it loses its powers.

CHILDREN

Don't bring children bad luck

No compliments

The widespread custom in Western countries of praising children's beauty and intelligence is ill-omened: it brings them bad luck, so be chary with your compliments.

If someone else praises your child

Thank them for the compliment but immediately touch wood or, if you can do so discreetly, make the sign of the cross. This will avert the omen.

It is also ill-advised

• To let a child adorn itself with jewellery belonging to its parents.

22

- To give a child presents which it cannot use until much later.
To do either is to tempt Providence.

Our advice

Refer to the words **BABY** and **CHRISTENING** to find out what is lucky or unlucky for children.

CHRISTENING

Don't spoil your child's christening

So that your child will profit fully from the omens associated with a christening, you must from the very start take the greatest care over the circumstances of this ceremony.

The church: avoid new ones

The christening should never be the first one to take place in a new church or at a new font: this is very unlucky.

Godparents: choose them carefully

Don't ask a pregnant woman to be godmother – this would be very unlucky for her.

Don't ask an engaged couple to stand as godparents – or their marriage will never take place.

Do try to have godparents who come from three different parishes – your child will live to a ripe old age.

The name

Never pronounce your child's first name before the christening. Not only would it take away much of the point of this naming ceremony, but it would expose him to risk. Until his name has been sanctified by the Church, it can be used against him in malicious spells. In addition: *don't* give your child any jewellery bearing his name before the christening; *don't* let his name be written on his hospital identity bracelet. Use the family name.

The baptismal water

When your child's head is sprinkled with the baptismal water don't under any circumstances wipe it off. This would be unlucky.

Good and bad omens

Observe your baby's behaviour during the ceremony.

It is a bad omen if he sneezes. Avert it by making the sign of the cross or touching wood, e.g. the nearest pew or chair.

It is a good omen if he cries, especially if it is when he feels the water on his face. This is a sign that 'the Devil is being driven out'.

Our advice

Don't be embarrassed by your baby's crying and wish he would 'shut up'. Soothe him by all means – but try to remember that this is *not* a social event which he is 'spoiling'. The sanctity of the rite is in no way affected by his crying.

Don't, on the other hand, pinch him deliberately (as some do) to make him cry. This is:

    a) unkind

and b) useless.

The omen must be unforced.

Baptize the child in the name of the family

Even if you're not religious, don't give your child his first name without carrying out a little ceremony to give meaning to the occasion. If he is not to enter the spiritual community of your faith, he should at least be made part of the spiritual community of the family.

Here is a little secular ritual which will allow you to give meaning to the first name you are giving to your child.

1. Have ready a glass of wine – otherwise the normal beverage of your country – also a piece of bread or a dish of whatever is the staple cereal.

2. Hand over the child to the godparents who will *together* hold it during this short ceremony.

3. The oldest man in the family then present – the father, grandfather, uncle or paternal great-uncle – will proceed to the baptism, using a form of words something like this: *'I, so-and-so (for example, John Bridges), as head of the Bridges family here present,*

admit you into our family community. You will bear the name of . . . (the first name of your child). *It is my hope that this forename will help you to carry the name of the Bridges proudly. I give you as godfather so-and-so, and as godmother so-and-so, and they will be responsible henceforth for supporting your parents in the heavy burden represented by the education they must give you, and for coming to your aid at any time your parents cannot for whatever reason do so themselves.'*

4. Taking the bread and the wine and offering them to the child, the grandfather (if it is he) will solemnly say: *'I offer you this food and this drink which you are yet unable to consume but which will be your food and drink, as you grow older. They represent the prosperity of our family. May fate and your life permit you one day to do likewise for those that follow you.'*

5. The grandfather will then take the child from the hands of the godmother and godfather, kiss him and lift him above his head, saying: *'To all of you, family and friends, I present . . . (first name of child) Bridges.'*

6. The godmother will then slip on to the child's arm a bracelet with his name engraved on it. The godfather will put round the child's neck a chain with a medallion bearing his name.

7. The child may then be put in the cradle or crib, leaving the family to celebrate with plenty to eat and drink.

It is essential to celebrate this happy event in style, so that the child may have a prosperous life later on.

Don't choose the godfather and godmother at random, because of a temporary friendship: their role should not cease on the day of the christening.

Our advice

Don't fail to take all these precautions: they alone will enable the adult man or woman to hold on to their luck whenever it comes their way.

CHRISTMAS PUDDING

Stirring the pudding: a wish will be granted

Mixing the Christmas pudding brings luck for the whole of the coming year.

Every member of the household should take a stir and secretly make a wish for the not too distant future: there's every chance that it will be granted.

For extra luck

Into the Christmas pudding you should stir:

a *silver coin* – to bring fortune to the finder

a *ring* – to bring a wedding

a *thimble* – to bring a life of single blessedness

Warning!
- The pudding must always be mixed clockwise.
- Do not tell anyone your wish or it will not come true.

CIGARETTES

Don't light three cigarettes with one match

You must never light three cigarettes with one match: misfortune is sure to fall on the person whose cigarette is the last to be lit.

You probably know the story

It was during the Boer War. One night, when the troops were encamped opposite each other, a soldier lit a cigarette. An enemy, seeing this tiny flame in the distance, loaded his rifle; then the soldier who was smoking lit a comrade's cigarette with the same light so that the enemy soldier had time to aim; finally, when the third smoker lit his cigarette, the enemy was able to fire and kill him. This is supposed to have happened several times.

Our advice

With one match: light one cigarette, then use that cigarette to light the other two.

With a lighter: light the first cigarette, put the lighter out and light it again for the other two.

CLERGYMAN

Meeting a clergyman brings bad luck

If you happen to meet a clergyman or priest: such an encounter is not a favourable one – far from it.

Note This does not mean that they themselves are ill-omened – simply that their religious function makes them messengers of fate. When you happen to meet them, the message they bring you – involuntarily – is of bad luck for the rest of the day.

It's easy to avert the omen

Avert the omen by:

1. touching one of your **AMULET(S)**; or
2. crossing your fingers; or
3. touching 'cold iron'.

Two special cases

The bad omen does not apply:

- if you know the clergyman or priest personally;
- if he is going into or coming out of a church.

COAL

Coal brings luck and protects you

Use coal as a talisman

A small lump of coal in one of your pockets or your handbag will bring you luck. It should be a piece that has been given to you or that you have found by chance.

27

Our advice

1. Take a small lump of coal, 1 or 2 cubic cm.
2. Make a small envelope of black silk.
3. Turn it inside out and rub the surface thoroughly with dry soap.
4. Reverse the silk envelope, so that the soapy surface is on the inside.
5. Slip the coal into the envelope.
6. Join up the envelope with one stitch.

Fortune may favour you

If you find a piece of coal as you are walking along a road or down the street, you should rejoice: Fortune is smiling on you. To preserve your luck you must pick up the coal and spit on it, throw it over your left shoulder, then walk on without looking back.

Note A wish made while you are doing this is certain to be fulfilled.

Don't leave your luck behind!

You may, instead of throwing the coal over your shoulder, pick it up and take it home. But, whether to throw it away or take it home, *do not fail to pick it up*. To leave it where it lies is to leave your luck behind.

The First Foot

Coal is one of the lucky gifts which the First Foot brings with him when he enters your house on New Year's morning as your first visitor. If there is no one you can ask to be your First Foot, you may still ensure your family's prosperity for the coming year by bringing in some coal as the first thing you do on New Year's Day.

Warning! The coal must be brought in through the front door, from outside. No luck follows if it is fetched from a basement or indoor cellar.

Our advice

Prepare a supply of coal just outside your front door on the previous night, so that you may be certain to perform this ceremony as the first thing you do.

(See also **NEW YEAR'S DAY**.)

COCK

The cock crows: a sign of fate

The crowing of the cock is always an omen

- If the cock perches on a gate to crow or crows at nightfall, he is forecasting bad weather the next day.
- If the cock crows at midnight, he is foretelling a death in the neighbourhood.
- If the cock crows near the front door or comes indoors at any moment during the day, he is announcing an unexpected visitor or a stranger. It is in your interest to be there to receive this visitor.

Our advice

If you are buying a cock for your poultry run, choose a white cock rather than a black one. A white cock brings good luck and protects the farm or homestead on which it lives.

Warning! It is extremely unlucky to kill such a cock.

COFFIN

Coffins are dangerous: even miniature ones

To have a miniature coffin in the house is ill-omened. In recent years, 'novelties' have been launched on the market: money-boxes, cigarette-boxes, drinks cabinets – all in the shape of coffins. All these articles are unlucky: to own and use them can only bring you trouble.

Don't hand over your clothes

In a number of countries, it is traditional to 'dress the corpse' as handsomely as possible for the funeral. In these distressing circumstances, a tie, jacket or some other article of clothing may be lacking.

29

Our advice

Never give away any of your clothes for this purpose: as they rot in the ground or are burnt, so your luck will gradually disappear.

COIN

A coin: a talisman for wealth

Carry a coin to increase your luck

There are two special sorts of coin which will increase your luck if always carried on you.

1. *A coin with a hole in it.* Coins which have been perforated accidentally are the most effective, failing this, use a holed coin such as the old French sou.
2. *A bent coin.* A bent coin *which you have found* brings you good luck: one you have bent yourself does nothing for you (see under **TALISMAN**).

Watch the moon

When you go out at night, always carry some loose change in one of your pockets. If you happen to notice as you are walking along that the moon is in its first quarter (the horns of the crescent pointing to the left ☾), turn the coins over without taking them out of the pocket. This will ensure your prosperity for the current month.

The cuckoo's call promises prosperity

If you hear the **CUCKOO** when walking in the woods, and have any loose change in your pocket, this is a fortunate sign. Turn it over and make a wish, and this will certainly be granted.

When you put on new clothes

When you are putting on a new garment for the first time, if it has a pocket, put a small coin into it at once. You will always have plenty of money whilst wearing it.

30

A coin can attract luck

If you discover in your purse a coin which was struck in the year you were born, get a jeweller to mount it on a ring or a pendant: for the rest of your life, it will bring you luck in every field.

Our advice

Look at the coins which pass through your hands. Maybe *you* will discover this rare specimen.

Warning! If you are sweeping your house and notice a coin lying in the dust, you *must* pick it up and put it in your purse or your pocket, even if it's only a small one. *Never throw it away.*

(See also **MONEY**.)

COLOURS

Favourable colours

It would be silly to attempt to classify colours as lucky and unlucky. A colour which is lucky for love may be ill-omened for business. Similarly a colour which is favourable for a child or an adolescent may prove to be ill-omened for an old man. By attempting to over-simplify the relations between colours and luck, one runs the risk of obtaining the opposite of the desired result.

White

Clothes

Good in all spheres of activity for men of power (financial, physical or spiritual).
Not recommended: for old men, young men, or women in their professional activities (unless they are very powerful, e.g. managing directors, senior civil servants).
Allowed: for women and girls who wish to use their helplessness to attract men.

Rooms and furniture

Kitchens, living-rooms, halls.

Blue

Clothes

Suitable for men of power, in all spheres of activity.
Light blue and bright blue recommended: for young men, tall men, athletes (=physical power).
Dark blue recommended: for men and women wielding political and financial power; all men until they reach middle age.
All blues allowed: for young blondes wishing to attract men through their fragility and childlike qualities.

Note Blue clothes protect children from bad luck, up to the age of three.

Rooms and furniture

Bedrooms, rest-rooms (for staff).

Green

Clothes

Recommended: for everyone involved in fishing, shooting, agriculture, mining, prospecting, pharmacology and homeopathic medicine. Green is especially good for pregnant women, growing children and people weakened by illness.
Forbidden: for people in industry, trade* and public relations.

Rooms and furniture

Bathrooms, swimming-pools.

Yellow

Clothes

Golden yellow recommended: for everybody under any circumstances, but never dress entirely in this colour.
Pale yellow forbidden: to everyone.

Rooms and furniture

Golden yellow: living-rooms, offices (except reception).
Pale yellow: lavatories only. Forbidden everywhere else.

* This includes farmers, miners and huntsmen while engaged in selling the products of their labours.

Red

Clothes

Good for everyone is a touch of red.
Recommended: for those engaged in industrial activities and the processing of raw materials.
Allowed (for seduction): red accessories (scarf, handkerchief) for dark men; red dresses for brunettes, or for tall or athletic women.
Forbidden (in this context): for fair men and blondes.

Orange

Clothes

Forbidden: orange-coloured clothes or clothes with touches of orange.

Exceptions: leisure and holidays, dances (brunettes only).

Rooms and furniture

Walls and furniture of offices, reception or shops. Rooms where private parties and dances take place.

Violet

Clothes

Touches of violet should be worn by commissioned and non-commissioned officers, leaders of men, job-hunters (looking for responsible posts).
Forbidden (for seduction): for both men and women.
Not recommended: for actors, acrobats or salesmen.

Brown

Ill-omened for everyone everywhere.

Exception: soldiers, miners and quarrymen at work.

Grey

Clothes

Lucky for everyone. Should be the dominant colour worn by anyone who needs to convince others or to be accepted by an audience.

Rooms and furniture

Libraries, music-rooms, exhibition and conference halls.

Pink
Clothes

Lucky for everyone, but always team it with other colours.

Rooms and furniture

Touches of pink in any room.

Black
Clothes

Neutral for everyone.

Rooms and furniture

Touches of black in a décor. But black-painted walls are forbidden: they absorb your vitality.

COMB

Don't pick up a comb

If you or someone else accidentally drops a comb – *don't pick it up.* This would be most unlucky.

Avert the omen by carefully treading or walking on the comb before you pick it up.

CROSS

Some crosses bring bad luck

All crosses made accidentally bring bad luck

- Knives crossed accidentally on a table.
- Tools which form a cross when dropped.

- Hands crossing in a group of people shaking hands.
- Forks and spoons crossed on a table.
- A bed forming a cross with the exposed beams of a ceiling.
- Crossed straws or branches in one's path.

All these are ill-omened. When you meet them, they take away your luck and increase your difficulties for about a week.

To avert these omens

Straighten out the cross and then follow the instructions below.

Cutlery and tools: uncross them immediately.

Crossed hands: say 'hello' or 'goodbye' a second time without crossing hands.

Straws or branches: uncross them, pick them up with your right hand and throw them over your left shoulder.

Bed forming a cross with a beam: move the bed so that it is parallel to the beams.

CROSSING THE FINGERS

Crossing the fingers

You cross your fingers by putting your second finger over your forefinger.

A. To attract luck in a lottery or at the roulette table, while the winning number is being drawn or the wheel is spinning.
B. To avert bad omens of all kinds.
C. And in every case where you suspect that a person you meet has the **EVIL EYE**.

CROSSROADS

Crossroads: places of ill-omen

Beware of crossroads

Try to avoid all remote and rarely frequented crossroads, including intersections of deserted streets, country roads, and mountain or forest tracks.

Especially malignant are:

- dirt or stone-paved roads or tracks;
- roads or tracks through a forest;
- roads or tracks crossing at perfect right angles.

When should you avoid these ill-omened spots?

Avoid crossroads when you are walking or riding. In a two- or four-wheeled vehicle, the metallic parts will protect you from evil and the advice below doesn't apply.

At all costs never stop!

Never stop in the middle of a crossroads and turn around to try and get your bearings.

Our advice

If you do not know your way, in order to find the road you should take, go round the crossroads without stopping.

Note Potentially dangerous but never ill-omened are *busy* crossroads, such as the crossings of main thoroughfares in towns and of main roads in the country. While on them you need not be afraid of any malign influences.

CUCKOO

The cuckoo, harbinger of spring

The first cuckoo of the year tells us that spring has arrived.

When you hear it affects your future

- Hearing the first cuckoo before 6 April is very unlucky.
- Hearing the cuckoo for the first time on 28 April is very lucky.
- Hearing the cuckoo for the first time after Old Midsummer Day (5 July) is very unlucky and may presage a death.

Note the direction from which the cuckoo calls

- If the first cuckoo-call you hear is coming from the right or from in front of you, this is lucky.
- If it comes from the left or behind you, it is unlucky.
- In whatever direction you are looking when you first hear the cuckoo call, there will you be a year from that day: if you are looking at the ground, you will be dead and buried before the year is out.

Take care what you do

Whatever you are doing when you hear the first cuckoo of spring governs your luck for the twelve months to come. It is particularly unlucky to be fasting or lying in bed, for this portends poverty and illness.

Our advice

As soon as you hear the first cuckoo, turn over whatever money you have in your pocket and this will bring you luck. If you make a wish at the same time, it will be granted.

DAYS OF THE WEEK

The days of the week: what you should always do

On Monday, the day of the moon

> do your washing
> have a bath
> wash your hair
> practise clairvoyancy
> draw the cards

make use of your intuition
till the soil

On Tuesday, the day of Mars

start a new job
take someone to court
have your debtors arrested
do business
eat plenty of red meat

On Wednesday, the day of Mercury

propose a purchase, sale or exchange
put in some advertisements
start a new course of medical treatment
see your doctor
start a new business
write your letters
ask favours

On Thursday, the day of Jupiter

take important decisions
accept a responsible post
take on or dismiss staff
reward or punish

On Friday, the day of Venus

have a flirtation
dance
and more . . .
do all your gardening

On Saturday, the day of Saturn

meditate
analyse your situation and that of your family
examine your conscience
rest
undertake a course of study

On Sunday, the day of the sun

Everything is allowed. Enjoy yourself!

What you should not do

On Monday

enter into commitments
ask favours
sign contracts
make promises

On Tuesday

cut your nails
undergo an operation
expose yourself to danger
wear a flower in your buttonhole

On Wednesday

make large purchases
wear gloves

On Thursday

start a new job, if in a subordinate position
send your children to a new school for the first time

On Friday

get married
start a new job
make a journey
go sailing
do any business
hold a meeting

On Saturday

leave hospital
carry out any activity with a utilitarian purpose

On Sunday

Nothing is forbidden on Sunday: it is the most favourable day of
the week.

Our advice

Follow these instructions carefully. They will enable you to 'tame' good luck.

DEATH

A death: necessary precautions

A death in the family

If a member of your family dies, you must immediately:

1. stop all the clocks;
2. cover the mirrors with black cloth, or turn them to the wall;
3. let the household fire go out;
4. open all windows and doors;
5. undo all locks and bolts, and untie every knot.

Important

Don't leave the dead person alone in the house – keep him company (you don't have to be in the same room).

Don't leave him in the dark – keep a candle or night-light burning.

Our advice

This is a time of uncertainty for the departing spirit. Give your family member all the help you can, apart from the last rites of his or her religion, by following these rules.

Warning! Don't restart the clocks and so forth until the funeral is over. But if there is an interval of some days between death and the funeral, you may rekindle the fire, and close the windows and doors.

DOG

Your dog: a faithful companion and a diviner too

Your dog gives you warning

- If it whines persistently for no good reason, it's a sign of misfortune coming to the family.
- If it barks for no apparent reason, it's warning you of the presence of evil spirits.
- If it howls in the night, it's foretelling a death or some calamity.

Any dog

- If it howls persistently in front of a house where someone is ill, that person will die. This omen is strengthened:
  a) if the dog belongs to someone in the house;
  b) if the dog is driven away, but returns and howls again.
- If any dog suddenly howls three times and falls silent, it is a sign that a death has just occurred nearby.

A strange dog

- If a strange dog comes to your house, it is a sign of new friendship.
- If a dog passes between a couple on their wedding day, it is a bad omen. To avert it, they must give each other a kiss.
- If you meet three white dogs together, this will bring you luck.
- If you meet a spotted or black and white dog on your way to a business appointment, your project will be successful.

Our advice: your dog recognizes your friends

If you have a dog, trust it to tell good friends from bad; if it always barks fiercely on the arrival of someone you know, it means that this person's visits are ill-omened for you.

On the other hand, the people your dog welcomes joyously are always luck-bearers.

Note Not all dogs are equally skilled in this respect. Dogs of certain breeds – watch-dogs, sheep-dogs or farm-dogs – are better than gun-dogs at telling good friends from bad ones and gun-dogs are better at it than lap-dogs.

Don't kill your dog or have it put down*

This is one of the most ill-omened acts a man can commit: it guarantees seven years' bad luck.

Only the vet, whose duty and function it is, escapes the ill luck, which in this case falls on those who have asked him to do it.

DREAM

A dream of love! A sure omen

Are you in love?

If you are, your greatest anxiety is to know whether your love is returned. The most significant presages of love are those which come to you in dreams.

Study your dreams

To start with, if you dream every night of the one you love, you should know that this does not prove anything regarding the love he or she has for you – but only that you are very much in love!

If you dream of a hare

Your love is returned, together with a powerful sexual desire. The erotic will then play a primary role in your future relations with your loved one. You have just met the man or woman with whom you will be able to realize most of your sexual fantasies.

Ladies: invite the man you love to your flat. Don't be afraid to make yourself seductive: if *you* have dreamt of a hare, don't expect *him* to make the running. In his dreams, he sees you as a courtesan and it's only if you behave like one that his love will be able to express itself.

Men: invite the woman you love to your home, rather than to a restaurant. See that the ambience is romantic: soft music, shaded lights, a delicious but light supper. Suggest dancing after the meal and, if she agrees, don't be shy.

---

* There is only one circumstance in which one can have a dog killed without risk to oneself. This is where euthanasia becomes necessary to relieve the animal of suffering, and the disease or affliction it has would in any case soon cause its death.

If you dream of a wolf, a star or a bird

The one you love shares your feelings but loves you in quite a different way. *She* is more wife than mistress, *he* more husband than lover – both look forward to a shared life or wish to start a home. If in your dream the wolf is caught in a trap, or the bird shot by a hunter, or if the star explodes or falls, this is a presage of your future relationship. You are the one who will be unfaithful or eventually leave.

Ladies: if you have dreamt of any of these things, it means that the man you love longs to protect you. Learn to act like a little girl with him and don't play the *femme fatale*. You will win him over by being naive, tender and a good housekeeper.

Men: be tender. Don't play the Don Juan: you would only frighten her.

If you dream of feet or of a sword

This foretells amorous conquests for you, and also tells you that someone loves you secretly. The presage is strengthened if you dream that you are the first to set foot in a newly discovered country or if you dream that whole populations submit to your sword. This dream indicates that the person who loves you secretly will reveal himself (or herself) and that you will make a conquest.

If you dream of fish

Your love is shared and the love which is felt for you is of the same nature as the love that you feel. Don't make any special effort; be content to be yourself with your beloved. Things will come about quite naturally.

If you dream of a great light

A great *amour passion* awaits you. This is true whether or not you are actually in love at the time.

If you are romantic and wish your love to be mingled with drama, and if the fear of losing your beloved increases the joy of being with him or her, go ahead and be happy: your desires will very soon be met.

If, on the other hand, you value your emotional stability, your job, your comfort and your family, concentrate as much as possible on your work and on your various obligations. Perhaps you will escape the anguish and the dramas of a great love (though you may long regret it). It is for you to choose.

If you dream of precious vases, of springs, streams, rivers or waterfalls

These pastoral images tell you that the one you love has an idealized love for you. He or she is in love with your elegance, your intelligence or your talent. In your lover's eyes, you are a god or goddess, and it is in listening to you, looking at you or even at your photograph that his or her love finds fulfilment. If you are content with this, then leave things as they are. But if you want platonic love to be changed to physical love, you will have to come down off your pedestal. You should, however, be warned that once you cease to be a god or goddess, it may be the end of the affair.

How to interpret these dreams

The presages which appear in dreams generally require the advice of a specialist for their interpretation. Only the power of love can inspire dreams so clear and detailed that everyone can interpret them without risk of error.

How to recognize a premonitory dream

If your dream is premonitory, on waking you will recall the significant image quite distinctly. Although the dream in question is far from being a nightmare and has not disturbed your feelings or your sleep, it has imprinted this image on your memory with the same power as the nightmare that wakes you in the middle of the night.

Make your dreams to order

Premonitory dreams can be spontaneous but there is also a way of inducing them. At night, before going to sleep, place under your pillow a photograph of your loved one – or something belonging to him or her. Try to forget this object and the expected dream will come during the night.

If the dream doesn't come the first night, it means that you haven't succeeded in forgetting the object completely. Leave it in its place and sleep on it without worrying any more about it. Forgetfulness will come the next night or the one after, and the dream you desire will come too.

DRESSING

Dressing to be lucky

To put on good luck
- Put your right arm first into any item of clothing.
- Put both legs into your trousers at the same time.
- Put your left sock or stocking on before your right.

(But see **SHOES**.)

Take care!

Don't sew on a button or carry out any other repair when you are actually wearing the garment.

Important

If you accidentally put on a garment inside out, this is very lucky. But leave it as it is, or your luck will be changed.
 The same applies if you put on odd **SOCKS AND STOCKINGS**.
 Conversely, if you do up buttons wrongly, you must correct the situation straightaway. (See **BUTTON**.)

Our advice

Follow our recommendations to the letter. In this way, you will be putting on the true armour of luck for the whole day.

ECLIPSE

An Eclipse: take care

Eclipse of the sun: eclipse of fate

The best omens lose their meaning during a solar eclipse.
 The effect is spread over seven days: it is apparent for three days before the eclipse and for three days after it.

During the seven days affected by the eclipse, nothing is good and nothing bad. There are no signs of fate.

Eclipse of the moon: definitely unlucky

Not only do good omens become inapplicable, but nothing favourable can occur during this period.

The influence of the eclipse likewise lasts for seven days: three days before and three days after.

Our advice

Keep calm. Don't undertake anything new during the seven days under the influence of a lunar or solar eclipse. Avoid meetings, new undertakings and anything that would alter your current situation: a change would not be to your advantage.

Note that eclipses are shown on the calendar.

EVIL EYE

Watch out for the Evil Eye

The Evil Eye is much more common than you might think. So *beware*!

How to recognize the Evil Eye

People:
    with eyes of different colours
    with eyes set deep in the head
    with eyes too close together
    with one eye lower than the other with squints
may have the Evil Eye and be able to 'overlook' those who accidentally cross them.

The involuntary Evil Eye

Note that possession of the Evil Eye is not necessarily voluntary. Some people are affected *against their will* with the ability to 'overlook' others.

46

Some animals and birds also have the Evil Eye

Creatures possessed of the Evil Eye include black cats, black sheep and rams, crows and all totally black birds, and magpies.

Warning! Never kill any of these creatures: this intensifies the misfortune.

Who is susceptible to the Evil Eye?

Everyone, including animals. Those most susceptible are:

children under seven
girls at the age of puberty
pregnant women
young couples during their first year of marriage
cattle and horses

Have you got the Evil Eye?

Yes, if:

- mayonnaise won't thicken when you are around;
- the plants in your borders never seem to grow;
- you start to lose regularly at games of chance, where before you were usually lucky;
- you feel fearful and anxious, without being able to say why.

No, if:

- mayonnaise and other sauces thicken properly;
- the plants in your house or garden grow normally;
- your luck at gaming, whether good or bad, remains exactly the same;
- you feel no anxiety or only anxiety whose causes you are aware of.

Our advice

If you meet a person you suspect of having the Evil Eye, cross your fingers until they have passed or spit on the ground as soon as they have gone. *Do not let them see you do this.*

In addition, always carry a protective amulet, such as a blue bead or a piece of red thread. The sign of the hand is especially powerful against the Evil Eye: when abroad look for manufactured amulets in the shape of a hand with the fingers spread or making the 'horns' (see **AMULET** and **HORNS**).

For the protection of children, see **UMBILICAL CORD**.

'FIG'

'Making a fig' to ward off the Evil Eye

How to 'make a fig'

Close the right fist, pushing the thumb out between the index and second fingers.

When and where should you 'make a fig'?

- In the direction of the person who wishes you ill or who brings you bad luck.
- In the direction of the horse who is going to beat the one you have put your money on.
- In the direction of a black cat or a crow, or any ill-omened creature.

Our advice

When you fig, bend your left arm under your right arm, your closed *left* fist touching the right forearm.

Be careful how you use it!

In some countries, for example Italy, 'making a fig' is not only a counter to the Evil Eye but an insulting sexual gesture. Be careful how and when you use it!

FINGER

Your finger: a pointer to your fate

Your fingers are indicative of your talents

- If you have long fingers, you are a spendthrift and will never save money.
- If you have a crooked little finger, you will one day be rich.
- If you have a forefinger as long as, or longer than, your second finger, you may be dishonest.
- If you happened to have been born with an *extra* finger, you will be lucky throughout your whole life.

Our advice: be observant

Always look at the fingers of the person you are talking to: this will tell you what sort of a person you are dealing with.

Don't forget

- A white spot on the *thumb-nail* means a present.
- A white spot on the nail of the *forefinger* announces the arrival of a friend.
- A white spot on the nail of the *second finger* is a sign that an enemy is coming.
- A white spot on the nail of the *fourth finger* means a journey.

FISHING

Fishing: how to be lucky

If you want luck to favour you when you go fishing,

Don't tempt fate!

Don't change your rod in the course of the day's fishing (unless you've broken it).

Don't put your landing-net in the water until a fish has taken the hook.

Don't sit on a lobster-pot or on an upturned basket when you're fishing.

Don't change a float which has served you well for a year for an improved and supposedly more effective one.

Your dress

White brings anglers bad luck. They should not wear white clothes.

If you're spinning, you must never hook the spoons on your hat.

Our advice

To have good luck when out fishing, spit on your hook before casting.

FLOWERS

Give flowers to cheer your nearest and dearest

Count the flowers in the bouquet

Make it a definite rule that you *never give an even number of flowers*: it brings bad luck. If, for example, you buy a dozen roses, don't hesitate to sacrifice one of them, so as to give only eleven.

Flowers, by all means, but what colour?

> red flowers – a passionate love
> pink flowers – a faithful love
> yellow flowers – disdain
> purple flowers – goodwill, consideration and respect

Hospital notes

If you are bringing flowers to a patient: *never bring red and white flowers mixed together in the same bunch*. This is a sign of a death in the ward, though not necessarily that of the person to whom you give them (see also **HOSPITAL**). Give instead red flowers alone to symbolize life, purple flowers to symbolize goodwill, or orange or flame-coloured flowers to represent vitality.

Our advice

Give flowers often: they are a symbol of happiness.

Danger when travelling

Never take flowers aboard an **AEROPLANE** or a ship. This would bring you bad luck. If you have a mixed bunch of red and white flowers, the risk is even greater.

Don't bring white flowers indoors!

Don't bring white flowers, especially those with heavy scents, into the house: they are omens of misfortune, sometimes even of death. Particularly unlucky are:

> white lilac

may (hawthorn blossom)
snowdrops

(See further under **HAWTHORN** and **LILY-OF-THE-VALLEY**.)

FOOTBALL

Football: subject to luck like everything else

If, on the way to the ground, you meet:

a black cat
a clergyman or priest
a beggar
a man with a limp
a woman with a squint

you haven't much chance of winning.

Avert the omen in all instances by immediately crossing your fingers to cancel it out (see under **CROSSING THE FINGERS**).

Good and bad omens

- If the band plays any wrong notes in your National Anthem, luck is with you.
- If the band plays any wrong notes in your opponents' National Anthem, luck is with them.
- If the band gets both National Anthems wrong, the omens cancel out.

It's also a bad omen if the supporters' bus is green.

FOUR-LEAFED CLOVER

The four-leafed clover: a lucky draw

A nod from fate

If you find a four-leafed clover, this foretells a long period of good luck.

52

Our advice

Dry the four-leafed clover between two sheets of blotting-paper. When dry, put it into a plastic bag or an envelope made of greaseproof paper and keep it in your wallet. It will be a powerful **TALISMAN**.

FUNERAL

A funeral: observe the omens

Some signs of great import

- If the sun is shining during the funeral, its light will shine most brightly on the face of the mourner who will be the next one to die.
- If rain falls during the funeral, it is a good omen for the dead man's soul.
- If there is an odd number of people present at a funeral, this is extremely unlucky: one of them will soon die.

When the funeral of a member of your family is delayed

If the funeral is postponed for any reason whatsoever, another death will take place in the family or in the neighbourhood within three months. *If the waiting-period includes a Sunday, the omen is certain and cannot be averted.*

Don't hold a funeral

On New Year's Day – or there will be one in the parish every month of the coming year.

On a Sunday – or three more burials will follow within the week.

Meeting a funeral

Meeting a funeral is unlucky, especially for brides and those setting out on a journey.

Avert the omen by turning and following the procession for a little way.

Preceding a coffin

Preceding a coffin on its way to the churchyard is extremely ill-omened – it signifies misfortune and even death.

Note Once the priest or clergyman has met the funeral procession, this omen no longer applies.

GARLIC

Garlic: protects you and your home

Hang garlic in your home

Garlic protects your house from misfortune and also protects your health. To benefit from its virtues, hang a bunch or a string of garlic in your kitchen or in your living-room. Suspend the bunch from the ceiling, hang the string on the wall. Used in this way, the garlic will protect you for one year.

Choose your garlic carefully

The best for the protection of the house has bulbs almost as big as one's fist – this is the sort sometimes called oriental garlic, though it grows in most parts of the world.

Our advice

If you cannot get fresh garlic, use dried. It is no less effective than fresh, although you must change it every three months, as there is no way of knowing how long it has been in stock, and when garlic is very dry, it loses its power.

During an epidemic, wear a necklace of garlic

To make such a necklace, you need:

1. a length of fine string, such as kitchen string;
2. a needle;
3. an odd number of cloves of garlic (three, five, seven, etc).

Method Thread the cloves on the string with the needle and secure each clove with two knots.

This necklace can be made with dried or fresh garlic. You must wear it every day under your clothes; at night, it should be hung in your bedroom near your bed. It should be renewed as soon as the cloves become very dry or begin to rot.

GLASS

Glass: a magical substance

Drinking-glass

If a wine-glass or tumbler begins to ring

This is a very bad omen: it denotes the death of a sailor or a wreck at sea.

Avert the omen by immediately placing a finger on the rim of the glass to stop it ringing.

Window-glass

Seeing the new moon through glass

It is unlucky to see the new moon for the first time through glass.

Avert the omen at once by crossing your fingers or touching wood.

Looking-glass

(See **MIRROR**.)

Our advice

Keep an eye on your diary or the newspaper, and when the new moon is due, be sure to go outside to see it for the first time.

GLOVE

Be careful if you drop one

If you drop a glove

Never pick it up yourself or bad luck will follow. It is better to lose the glove.

But if someone else picks up your gloves and returns them to you

This is a lucky sign. You may expect a delightful surprise.

Avoid bad luck

If you leave your gloves at a friend's house, don't have them handed back to you at the door or you will never return there. Go into the house and sit down before picking up the gloves, and put them on when you are again standing. This will cancel out the bad luck.

GOOD FRIDAY

Good Friday: auspicious or inauspicious?

Unfavourable for some things

In theory, Good Friday is an inauspicious day on which it is important not to perform actions which symbolically re-enact the Crucifixion, e.g.

> *cutting* hair
> shoeing horses or doing anything involving *nails*

Note It is also unlucky to do the washing or sweep the house (see **BROOM**).

Favourable for others

In spite of its generally unfavourable character, Good Friday is the best day of the year for:

56

- baking (see **BREAD**);
- sowing parsley;
- weaning a baby.

Warning! Sowing parsley on any other day of the year will bring about a death.

Our advice

Do your utmost to wean your baby on Good Friday. It will give him every chance of a happy life.

GRAVEYARD

Do not meddle with graveyards

To plough up a graveyard: extremely ill-omened

At all costs you should avoid ploughing up ground which has previously been used as a graveyard or cemetery. Crops sown on such land will never thrive and ill luck will come to the family of the ploughman or the farmer who ordered it to be done.

Don't use tombstones for building or other purposes

Don't use bits of tombstone to build your house – if you build death into it, it will be unlucky and may even collapse.

Don't use broken tombstones for paths or roads – accidents will happen.

Warning! These rules apply just as much to ancient pagan cemeteries as to Christian ones: it is most ill-advised to plough out or otherwise destroy barrows, or re-use standing stones in field-walls or as gateposts.

Respect the dead and you have nothing to fear

Graveyards are not in themselves ill-omened places, as long as you bear certain rules in mind.

- It is unlucky to walk or tread on a grave, especially if it is that of an unbaptized child.
- It is very unlucky to take a dead body out of its grave, whether as the result of an exhumation order or simply to place it in another tomb. Disaster and even death will befall the dead person's family.
- It is both unlucky and dangerous to disturb any grave, ancient or modern. The consequences may range from insomnia to haunting.*

HAIR

A haircut: think of the moon

Keep your hair healthy

Your hair is important. It helps to maintain your vitality.

How to have your hair cut

Cutting the hair increases its vitality. This statement is only true for fourteen days in each month: between the new moon⬤and the full moon ☽.

In the fourteen days which follow the full moon, to have one's hair cut diminishes its power.

Our advice

Have your hair cut in the morning of the third day preceding the full moon. This is the most auspicious time. On the calendar, the full moon is shown thus: ☽.

* There is also the legal aspect. People whose jobs make it quite likely that they will one day accidentally disturb a grave (e.g. roadbuilders and construction workers) should remember that they *must* report the finding of human remains, ancient or otherwise immediately to the police. Note that the ill-luck accruing from such a disturbance seems to be passed on – not apparently to policemen, but to archaeologists.   Ed.

HAND

Your hand: a key to your character

Warm hands are not the sign of an amorous disposition, as some declare. On the contrary, *cold* hands indicate a *warm* heart.

Your hand gives you warning

If the palm of your *right hand* itches, you will be getting some money. If it's the *left hand* that itches, be ready to pay some out (see **ITCHING**).

Our advice

Rub your palm on wood for luck in both cases.

HAWTHORN

Hawthorn: a magical tree

The hawthorn is a magical tree which from ancient times has been used to defend the house against ghosts and evil spirits.

The hawthorn wards off lightning

The hawthorn will ward off lightning if you:

1. plant a hawthorn tree near your house; or
2. nail a branch of hawthorn to your door; or
3. hang a hawthorn ball in your kitchen.

To make a hawthorn ball

A. Tie short twigs of hawthorn on to a framework of chicken wire, or poke them through a round potato, an old rubber ball or a lump of 'oasis', first making a secure hanging loop by tying string to the wire or running it right through the 'oasis', potato or ball.
B. Add some mistletoe for good measure (another magical plant – see **MISTLETOE**).

59

C. Hang the ball up in your kitchen or main living-room.
D. At five o'clock on the morning of New Year's Day, take the old hawthorn ball out into your garden and burn it.
E. While it is burning, make a new ball and hang it in the same place, to protect your house during the coming year.

Note   It is luckiest if you gather the hawthorn from the wild, not from your own garden.

Our advice

If in your garden there is a spot newly dug or sown, this is the best place to burn the hawthorn ball – your new crop will certainly grow!

Hawthorn blossom: lucky or unlucky?

Before the calendar reform of 1752, May Day (1 May) fell eleven days later than it does now, when the hawthorn was in blossom – hence its name of 'may'. 'Bringing in the may' on May morning to decorate the house both inside and out, and to bless and protect it, was the custom. Now attitudes to may inside the house are very different.

May is lucky

• On the Continent, especially in sick-rooms, where it speeds recovery.
• In some parts of England, where it is brought into the house as a charm against lightning on Ascension Day.

May is unlucky

In most places in the British Isles, where may, like other white flowers (see under **FLOWERS**), is extremely unlucky if brought inside the house.

Our advice

Do not risk breaking this taboo, but play it safe and follow the general rule: *don't bring may into the house, or your mother is sure to die.*

HEALTH

Never say, 'I'm very well!'

If you are asked, out of politeness or affection, for news of your health, never reply that you are 'very well'. This kind of statement inevitably attracts illness or accidents.

Our advice

Dodge this purely formal question by returning it smartly to the enquirer.

HEARSE

Meeting a hearse: an evil omen

To meet a hearse is always unlucky (see **FUNERAL**). The omen is at its worst if the hearse is *empty*.

Note This omen only applies when you meet the hearse coming towards you. In all other cases, to pass or to see a hearse has no particular significance.

HEARTH

Fire: a symbol of life

The holy element of fire is a symbol of light and life. In olden days, when the hearth was in the middle of the room, the household fire was physically and spiritually the centre of its life, and for this reason was never let go out.

Our advice

Unless you have a closed stove, this is impracticable today, but even an ordinary modern side-hearth may be consecrated. Do this by lighting it for the first time after moving with an ember from the fire in your old house.

Warning! To maintain its sacred character, the fireplace must be kept spotlessly clean.

Avoid misfortune

Don't poke someone else's fire – the only person who may do so with impunity is a friend of at least seven years' standing.

Don't lend or borrow fire – if you must do so, follow the conditions for **SALT**.

Don't move fire from room to room – this is just as unlucky.

Don't give fire of any sort – including a light for someone's cigarette – out of the house on New Year's Day. To disobey this rule will bring a death in the family within twelve months.

Avert the omen If, for some reason, fire must be given out of the house on this day, ask for a trifle such as a pin to be given in return – this will avert the omen.

The fire in your grate foretells the future

Quarrels – the fire will not start in the morning; or roars up the chimney.

A parting – when the fire burns only on one side or in two quite separate parts.

A death – when the fire burns hollow, resembling a grave.

Good news – a cluster of bright sparks on the chimney-back.

Bad news – a cluster of *dull* sparks on the chimney-back.

A stranger – a smoky film on the bars of the grate.

Frosty weather – if the flames are blue or unusually bright.

Omens from coals and cinders

- A lump of coal that spits and hisses foretells quarrels – avert the omen immediately by breaking up the coal with a poker.
- A coffin-shaped cinder flying out of the grate foretells a death.
- An oval cinder shaped like a cradle flying out of the grate foretells a birth.

- A live coal falling out of the grate at someone's feet betokens a wedding.
- A live coal flying out at any person shows that he or she has an enemy.

HORNS

Be extremely careful

Making horns is a gesture which not only wards off the **EVIL EYE** but is an insult signifying cuckoldry – so use with discretion!

How to make horns

Close your hand, folding in the middle and ring fingers against the palm. Keep these two fingers down with your thumb. Keep the forefinger and the little finger extended in line with the wrist.

Horns are always made with the right hand

It is a mistake to make horns with both hands or just with the left hand. There are only three proper ways of making horns.

A. By simply closing your hand as indicated above. Use this, for example, to avoid being pushed around.
B. By making horns as above, but accompanying this gesture with a backwards and forwards movement of the hand in the

63

direction of the person at whom it is aimed. Use this for light-weight ill wishes (e.g. 'Go and jump in the lake!').

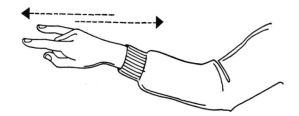

C. By bending your left arm in front of your face and making horns over the top of the arm. Use this to call down a curse equivalent to the one which has just been called down on you.

Who should you make horns at?

• Anyone who ill-wishes you by saying, 'Go to the Devil!', 'Drop dead', and so forth.
• Anyone who tries to push you around, either by tone of voice, look or words.
• Anyone who has the Evil Eye.

Our advice

When you make horns, remember that you are returning an ill wish.

HORSESHOE

The horseshoe: lucky – but not always

The horseshoe derives its beneficent power

From its shape – like a crescent moon.
From the material of which it is made – 'cold iron', a magical substance.

The best horseshoes

There is no substitute for a genuine iron horseshoe: imitation horseshoes and the miniatures on key-rings or sold as bracelet 'charms' have no power whatsoever.

A used horseshoe is better than a new one; and a horseshoe cast from *the near hind leg of a grey mare* is extra specially lucky.

If you find a horseshoe in the road

Fortune has indeed favoured you: this is a very good omen.

Warning! You must not pass by the horseshoe without paying it some attention. You may either:

1. pick it up and spit on it, at the same time making a wish, then throw it over your *left* shoulder and walk away without looking back; or
2. take it home and nail it over the door to your house.

How to get a horseshoe

Today, finding a horseshoe is a fairly unusual occurrence, so go to a riding stable, find out who shoes the horses, and ask him for a used shoe.

Where to fix the horseshoe

The horseshoe is meant to protect the whole house or bring it luck. It must therefore be fixed on the *outside*, over the door or on the threshold. To fix it inside the house is unlucky.

How to fix the horseshoe

To protect the house: fix it with the points downwards.

To bring good luck to the house: fix it with the points upwards, so that the luck will not 'run out'.

1. *To bring good luck*

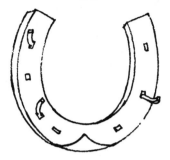

2. *To protect*

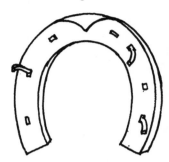

The horseshoe nails

- A horseshoe is particularly lucky if nailed to a door or threshold *with its own nails.*
- Fix the horseshoe with an *odd* number of nails: three or five, never two or four.

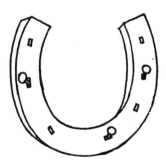

HOSPITAL

Hospital: when you enter and leave is important

If you have to go into hospital

- If you can choose the day you go into hospital, go in on a *Wednesday*.

66

- If you have to have an operation, refer to the entry on **MOON** when choosing the date.

When you are in hospital

- If someone gives you a bunch of red flowers, this is a good omen. Keep them in your room.

   Exception If you have just had an operation, give the bouquet to the hospital chapel.
- If someone gives you white flowers, this is a bad omen (see **FLOWERS**).
- If someone gives you red and white flowers mixed, this is a very bad omen (again see **FLOWERS**).

Avert the omen in both cases by giving the flowers to the chapel.

Leaving hospital

If it is suggested that you should leave hospital on a Saturday, refuse and don't leave until the Monday. *If you leave hospital on a Saturday, you will soon be back.*

HOUSE

When you move into a new house

We have described numerous ways of protecting your house from ill-fortune. To get all the luck on to your side, follow the instructions below.

Before moving your furniture into the house

1. Bring into the house a box or bucket of coal and a plate of salt.
2. Take a new broom and sweep the whole house clean (as explained under **BROOM**).

   You can now move in your furniture and possessions.

As soon as you are settled in

Fix something which protects against ill-fortune on the outside of the door or on the lintel (see **HAWTHORN, HORSESHOE, SICKLE**), and hang a bunch or string of garlic inside the house (see **GARLIC**).

Start on the right foot

Enter the house with your *right foot before your left*, particularly if you are a bride coming to your new home for the first time. To enter a house with the left foot foremost is unlucky.

Our advice: for your pets

Rub the underside of the paws of your cats and dogs with butter. Licking off the butter will stop them wanting to go back to their old home.

IDIOT

An idiot brings good luck

The simple-minded and the mentally retarded are real harbingers of luck. Their innocence causes them to be led or directed involuntarily by unseen powers.

Meeting one of them on your way to a rendezvous (of whatever kind) or on setting out on a journey is always a sign of good luck.

ITCHING

An itch is a warning

Your itchings are signs of fate

When you start to itch, it's always the omen of some unexpected event. On the *right side* of your body, it's always a favourable sign, but on the *left side*, an unfavourable one.

Some omens from itching

- If the palm of your *right hand* itches, you will soon be getting money. If it is the left hand, you will be paying some out.
- If your *right ear* itches, someone is speaking well of you, but if it is your left ear, they are speaking ill.

- If your *right eye* itches, you will get a pleasant surprise, but if the left one does so, a disappointment.
- If your *eyebrows* itch, expect a visitor.
- If the *soles of your feet* itch, you will soon tread strange ground.

Our advice

Your body may sometimes start to itch just when you are tempted to agree to a proposal.
    If the itch is on the right, *accept*.
    If it is on the left, *refuse*.

JEWELLERY

Jewellery: favourable or unfavourable?

Some pieces of jewellery are favourable, others unfavourable, depending upon whether or not you are in harmony with them.

Favourable jewellery

A piece is favourable if, when you wear it:

- your appointments work out better than expected;
- you feel in charge;
- your luck seems in top gear;
- chance and circumstance seem to work in your favour;
- you feel 'on the ball', brisk and efficient.

Our advice

Even if they are not very valuable, treasure such pieces: to lose them, sell them or give them away would destroy your good luck.

Unfavourable jewellery

A piece is unfavourable if, when you wear it, you notice that:

- your appointments lead to nothing;
- you're continually falling ill;
- your usual luck seems to have deserted you;

- events appear to be ganging up on you;
- you're less 'on the ball', less brisk and efficient.

Our advice

Give it away or sell it to a museum or to a collector. This is the best way to destroy its malign influence.

Copies of jewellery

Bad luck always pursues the owner of a piece who makes up a copy which doesn't follow the original design exactly.

JOURNEY

A journey: better safe than sorry

Don't look back

If you are leaving your house to go on a journey, *don't look back*. To do so is ill-omened and brings bad luck, lasting for the whole of the journey.

Don't retrace your steps

Have you left something behind in your own house or at your friends'? If so, *don't go back to look for it*: this ill-omened act would increase the risk of accidents, breakdowns, delays and difficulties.

Our advice

1. Go back into the house.
2. Sit down as soon as you are inside.
3. Count up to nine (some people count to ten or twelve).
4. Then pick up the object and leave with an untroubled mind. You have nullified the omen.

If your friends are leaving, give them a 'good luck' insurance policy

- When your friends leave your house, don't stand waving goodbye until the last moment, or you may never see them again.
- When you are seeing them off by car or train, don't watch the vehicle until it disappears from view, or bad luck will certainly follow.

Our advice

Say a hearty goodbye to your friends, then turn away while they are still visible.

JUSTICE

Justice: get luck on your side

Going to court

If you have to answer a writ or if you are bringing an action yourself, it is essential that you should:

A. *Before going into court*

Wash and dress with special care, choosing clothes that are impeccable but not ostentatious, e.g. a grey suit, with a pink or sky-blue shirt (or blouse) and tie.

Note If you wield spiritual or temporal authority, wear only grey – very discreet.

B. *In court*

Put your point of view in a clear and concise manner. Your bearing, intonation and eyes will all be important factors.

To increase the potency of your luck

Go into court without having breakfasted or taken a meal.

Our advice

If you have to rely entirely on the judge's clemency:

1. It is essential that you wear only white or blue.
2. Take a key with you: it is by far the best **TALISMAN** for helping you win your case.

KEY

The key: a powerful amulet

Your keys speak to you

*   If you drop your keys, this means something unpleasant will happen.
*   If you lose your keys, this means a death.

Keys as amulets

All keys are **AMULET(S)** and can be used against the **EVIL EYE**, except flat ones, such as Yale keys and other keys of a non-traditional shape.

The most powerful keys

The most powerful are old iron keys: the older a key, the greater its power to ward off evil.

Iron keys should be kept in the right-hand trouser pocket or in a handbag.

When touching a key to ward off evil, grasp its stem in your right hand.

Our advice

Jewel-case keys made of gold or silver, or even of copper or brass, are very effective. Wear them on a chain. To ward off evil, it is enough to touch them *with the second finger of the right hand*.

KISSING

Kissing: a most important matter

A beneficent kiss

If a child has just been introduced to you and kisses you spontaneously, this is an excellent forecast of long life. What is more, if you have just met with a bad omen, it's wiped out by the child's kiss.

Warning! Beware of the unwilling kiss: if a child does not want to kiss you, don't on any account force it to. If the parents insist and a kiss is then given, this is a very bad omen for your future.

Avert this omen by blowing immediately into your cupped hands (as if to warm them). This is the only way to ward off this bad omen.

The kiss and the present

If you have just given someone a present and he or she kisses you immediately after receiving it, this is a sign that the present you have just given forms a new bond between the two of you.

Note This omen is only effective if the person in question has really *seen* the object you have just given. If he or she kisses you before the parcel is unwrapped, the kiss is not an omen.

The maleficent kiss

There's only one and it's the kiss on the cheek given by someone standing behind you.

There is no effective way of exorcising this omen.

Our advice

Don't trust anyone who kisses you in this way, even if they are closely related to you.

KNIFE

Your knife: a talisman

If you use it regularly or usually carry it about with you, your knife can be both a **TALISMAN**, bringing good fortune, and an **AMULET**, warding off bad luck.

Note The knife shares this property with other cutting tools (see **AXE**).

Use of the knife-talisman

A knife is a protection against ill-fortune of many kinds.
- Stuck into the door, it will protect your house from evil influences.
- Stuck into the mast of a fishing-boat, it will bring it luck at sea.

Your knife: highly personal

If your knife is a very personal possession, always carried with you, it will have become imbued with your essential life-force. In this case it may function as an oracle when you are absent from home to tell people how you are.

What to do

If you are to be absent from home for a long period, i.e. several months or years, hang your knife up in the house before leaving.
- If the blade stays bright, you are safe and well.
- If it becomes dull, you are in danger or ill.
- If it rusts or breaks, this is an extremely bad omen – your family should expect to hear the worst.

Note As with all oracles – use your common sense. If the knife rusts unexpectedly quickly, it may simply be that your house is damp.

74

The knife is a dangerous object

This applies even to table-knives.

Don't make toast on the point of a knife. This brings misfortune on the house.

Don't cross the knives when laying the table, or lay one across a fork. Quarrels will follow, unless you avert this omen by straightening them immediately.

Don't leave a knife on the table overnight: if you do so, a burglar may enter the house.

Don't spin a knife on a table: this is generally unlucky.

Exception To find out if your future wife or husband will be fair or dark, spin a white-handled table-knife on the table. If it falls with the *blade* towards you, he or she will be *dark*; if with the *handle*, he or she will be *fair*.

If you want to give a knife as a present

When given as a present, knives sever friendship or love, so if you are giving one to someone, ask for a small coin in exchange.

The value of the coin is immaterial, so long as it *is* a coin – a bank-note will not do.

LADDER

The ladder is ill-omened

Don't defy the ladder

Don't walk under a ladder.

Don't reach for anything or hand over anything between the rungs of a ladder.

Both these actions are very unlucky.

Note Defying the ladder does not entail a long – or short – period of bad luck but a blow of fate which may fall at any moment.

To avert the omen

If you have accidentally defied the ladder:

1. cross your fingers until you meet a dog (on or off the lead); or,

2. maintain absolute silence until you have seen a four-legged animal of any sort; or,

3. spit three times through the rungs of a ladder, or once over your left shoulder; or,

4. spit on your shoe and walk straight, taking care not to look back until the wet mark has dried.

Our advice

If you have to work standing on a ladder, stand on an even rung (counting the rungs from the bottom).

Uneven rungs of a ladder are ill-omened.

LADYBIRD

The ladybird: harbinger of good luck

The ladybird is a beneficent insect. When it alights on you, it heralds either good luck or the end of your troubles. The most favourable sign is when it alights *on your hand* or *on your clothes*.

Pay attention to the ladybird

If a ladybird alights on you, observe it carefully and count its spots.

- The darker its overall colour, the better the luck it brings.
- The more spots the better: each represents one month of happiness for you.

Important

If the ladybird alights on you, it *must* be allowed to fly away of its own accord.

Never knock or brush it off, as this would be to drive away your good fortune.

You may, however, gently blow the ladybird away, if you first recite the formula:

> Ladybird, ladybird, fly away home.
> Your house is on fire and your children all gone.

Warning! Never kill a ladybird. This is a disastrous omen.

Our advice

If you accidentally kill a ladybird:

1. bury it carefully;
2. stamp on its grave three times;
3. recite the 'house on fire' formula.

This will avert the omen.

LAMB

What fate has in store for you

A lamb makes a prognosis of the coming twelve months

The first lamb you see in spring will tell you how the next twelve months will go.

- If its head is turned towards you, the coming year will be good.
- If its head is turned away from you, the coming year will be bad.

Special cases

- If you have money in your pocket when you see the first lamb of the year, this is a very good omen. Turn it over at once, and you will never be short of cash in the next twelve months.
- If the first lamb you see is black, this is doubly lucky: any wish you make now will be fulfilled.

For farmers

If the first-born lambs of the year are white twins, they will bring good fortune to your whole flock.

LEAP-YEAR

Leap-year: lucky year

All calendars require that, at regular intervals, we add to the year a certain period of time to maintain the calendar months' harmony with the cosmic order. Man has always attached a special significance to these 'compensatory' days.

Leap-years are favourable to all new undertakings, to changes in your life or profession.

Any undertaking which starts on 29 February has an excellent chance of success.

Similarly for your child, if it is conceived or born on that date.

LETTER

Signs that a letter is coming

- If a moth flies towards you.
- If your nose itches.
- If you have a white spot on the fingernail of your ring finger.
- If there is a bright spark in the wick of the candle.
- If you sneeze on a Wednesday.
- If a spider comes down at the end of its thread in front of your eyes.

To get a letter

- If you find a hairpin, hang it up on a nail and you will soon get a letter.
- If you and another person both speak at once, get him or her to pinch you: a letter will then arrive.

Your dreams warn

To dream of posting an unsealed letter means that your secrets are known.

Be careful!

Never put a letter in your sweetheart's left hand, or your love will come to an end.

Never burn a love-letter: this is to burn up your love.

Our advice

For your letters to have more impact, use a different pen or pencil for each type of letter.

Keep at least: one pen for business letters;
one pen for love-letters;
one pen for protest letters.

LIFT

The lift foretells your future

If you are stuck in a lift, it means that you will be stuck for a while in your career or your studies.

Three possibilities

• If you are freed by someone sending the lift up one or more floors, the difficulties you encounter will only be temporary ones.

• If you are freed by someone sending the lift down to the ground floor, you will encounter difficulties throughout your studies or your career.

• If you are let out of the cabin by the safety-hatch, you will probably make a change of subject in your studies or change your occupation. This is not necessarily a bad omen.

Avert the omen by going up by the stairs to the floor you intended to reach in the lift, taking good care not to stumble (see under **STAIRS**).

Pensioners only

For you, the lift breaking down is not a bad omen. It means that you will have a long life.

LILY-OF-THE-VALLEY

An ill-omened flower

Don't bring lilies-of-the-valley into the house. Like other white flowers they are unlucky (see **FLOWERS**).

Don't give a bunch of lilies-of-the-valley to a friend: they will destroy your friendship.

Don't plant a whole bed of lilies-of-the-valley: this always brings misfortune.

Our advice

If you want this fragrant flower in your garden, plant a single clump of crowns in a cool shady corner and leave it there. It will spread quickly of its own accord.

LOAN

A loan: six inauspicious days

During the six days of the year, bad luck attends all those who lend or borrow money, particularly (though not exclusively) affecting their financial affairs.

When neither to lend nor borrow

Don't borrow money on 1, 2 or 3 February, or on 29, 30 or 31 March. If you are foolish enough to do so, you may be sure that you will be unable to repay it.

Don't lend money on those days either, as you will have little chance of getting it back.

Our advice

If on one of the inauspicious days you are obliged to assist a friend or a member of your family financially, *give* him or her some money. This gift, even if very small, will bring you good luck for the year.

LOVE

Love: make it last

Love

There are certain covenants which can prove extremely powerful because they unite two human beings from within, awakening a need one for the other. They are like magic spells of mutual love. Here are two covenants which are particularly effective.

Carve your initials

This is a magic act, which has to be performed according to a rite with very precise rules.

1. Choose a young tree, on which no one has carved his initials before.
2. Do the carving with a new knife, bought specially for the occasion.
3. When you have finished carving, bury your knife at the foot of the tree, cover up the hole and make love on that spot.

Under these conditions, and only under these conditions, will your love grow with the tree.*

Our advice

Each should pull a leaf off the tree and keep it as a **TALISMAN**, in a medallion worn around the neck.

A covenant for your heart

Go to a remote place, either in the open country or an isolated cottage, but any house will do, provided it has a fireplace.

Requirements

1. A photograph of each of you.
2. Nine rusty nails.
3. A bottle of good wine.

* Conservationists please note: this may be good for lovers, but it is very bad for the tree. Cuts in its bark will expose it to attack by micro-organisms and insect pests.   Ed.

4. A wine-glass (crystal if possible).
5. Some dry kindling for the fire.

Note If you are indoors, begin by switching off all the lights. The fire alone should give you enough light. If you are in the open country, the light of the moon and the stars will not affect the operation. *On no account use a torch.*

Procedure

A. Light the fire.

B. As soon as it begins to burn, place the two photos together vertically, face to face, as if for a kiss.
   Madam: Hold the photos in this position between the thumb and forefinger of your *left* hand, your thumb *on your own picture*, your fingers at the *top*.
   Sir: You should also hold the photos between thumb and forefinger, but with your *right* hand, your thumb on your own picture, your fingers at the *bottom*.

C. Now fasten the photos together with the nine nails.
   Madam: Take the first nail and join the photos, piercing your own and then your lover's in one single action.

82

Sir: Do likewise with the second nail, again piercing your own photo.

D. When you have fixed in the nine nails, in a single gesture throw the photos into the fire, saying: 'May the secret of our relationship be entrusted to the element Fire.' Then, side by side, watch the photos burn.

E. As soon as they have been destroyed, fill the wine-glass.

F. Each of you now take a piece of kindling from the fire and plunge the burning end into the wine-glass to extinguish the flame.
Sir: Now take a sip of wine.
Madam: Take *two* sips of wine, then hurl the glass down in front of the fire.

Warning The wine-glass *must* break so that it can never be used again.

Our advice

If you are out of doors and the earth is soft, put a flat stone in front of the fire, so as to be certain that the glass will break.

If you do not want your love to last for ever

If you're unsure and afraid to commit yourselves indefinitely, here is a covenant to suit your requirements. It is effective for only three years, but, when this period is up, there is nothing to prevent your renewing it for another three years if you feel so inclined.

Requirements

1. An unglazed earthenware jug, large enough to be held by four hands.
2. A pure silk square, big enough to tie you both together at the waist.

Procedure

A. Stand face to face, with your bodies touching.
   Sir: You are holding the scarf.
   Madam: You are holding the jug.

B. *Sir:* Now tie the scarf around both your waists, as tightly as possible.

C. *Madam:* Lifting the jug in both hands, raise it carefully above your head and tell your lover to place his hands on it.

D. Once you both have hold of the jug, hurl it to the ground so that it breaks.

E. As soon as it shatters, you, Sir, undo the scarf and give it to your lover. She must keep it as long as your relationship lasts.

The rite is completed. Your relationship will last at most for the number of years equal to the number of broken pieces on the ground.

A dangerous secret

If you are really in love and 'ready for anything', here is an extremely powerful rite: a Blood Wedding. Because of its fabulous power and the rigid bonds it forges between two people, we expressly advise you not to perform it. None the less, since we live in a free world, we consider it our duty to give you the exact details of the procedure. You are free to enslave yourself if you so wish.*

Requirements

A razor blade.

Procedure

A. Take the razor blade and make a light cut on your forearm, about 5 cm from the wrist, males on the *right* arm, females on the *left*. (Make the cut on the top of your forearm, not on the inside.

---

* And to give yourself blood poisoning. Do be careful! Ed.

There is no point in cutting deeply into the skin: a single drop of blood is sufficient.)

B. Then make a similar cut on your lover's *opposite* arm, right for male and left for female.

C. As soon as a drop of blood has formed, hold your arms together, blood on blood, for at least one minute.

Once you have completed this rite you will be doubly united,

spiritually, through the mingling of your blood, the vehicle of the soul;

sensually, through the common acceptance and sharing of pain.

Note You can keep the razor blade you have used as a **TALISMAN** or you can throw it into the fire and with this gesture make the whole world a witness to your Blood Wedding.

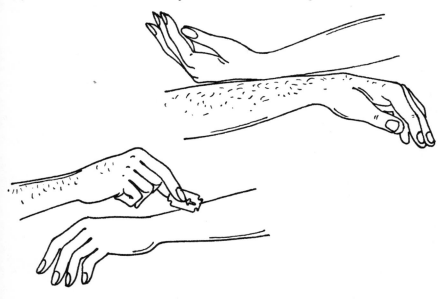

Our advice: think carefully!

This sort of covenant is the most powerful there is. Only a magician can loose this bond. This is both its attraction and its danger. Even if the lovers make each other unhappy, the blood-tie is so strong that they will remain together in their sorry state and be unable to do without each other. It is the only bond which can unite two people indissolubly. Therefore reflect carefully before entering into it and only perform the rite after much serious thought.

Keep it a secret

These covenants can complete a civil marriage or a church wedding, but they are also useful if you don't wish – or are unable – to be lawfully wedded. You can be united with your lover in this way under the very nose of your family and friends.

Warning! Never shout your good fortune to all and sundry. In love, secrecy is a primary rule. The fewer people know of your happy state, the more chance it has of lasting.

Our advice

Never give imitation jewellery or your love may turn out to be equally a sham. Love can be symbolized by many objects: a lock of hair, a statuette, a drawing and, perhaps best of all, something you have made with your own hands.

LUCK

How to attract good luck

First method: whether you are a Christian or not, make the sign of the cross

But when you make it, cross your second finger over your forefinger. This gesture has a significance which extends beyond the confines of Christianity. In making it, you are placing yourself favourably on to the world's axis (at the cardinal points) and achieving universal harmony. The cross must be made downwards and from left to right. You must touch your forehead, your solar plexus, your left shoulder and your right shoulder, in that order.

Our advice: make the sign of the cross of power

In the same way (middle finger crossed over forefinger), make successive crosses on your forehead, your mouth and your heart – this is even more effective. You must trace out the arms of the three crosses fully (as if with a piece of chalk).

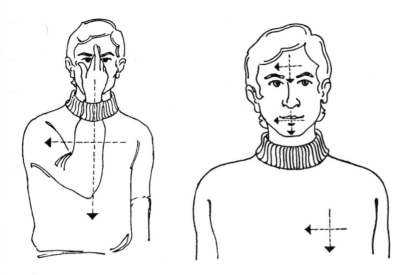

Second method: make horns behind your back

Place your right hand on your spine, level with your tailbone: the back of your hand must be touching it. Double your middle and ring fingers into the palm of your hand and lock them into position with your thumb. The two free fingers (the little finger and the forefinger) should point at right angles to your spine.

Third method: mark out a magic circle

Mark it out round your chair or round the place where you are going to sit, if local custom decrees that you sit on the ground.

Carefully follow the method below:

1. Choose your place.
2. Sit down.
3. Get up, and taking one step forward at a time mark out a circle of about 60 cm diameter with your feet, in a clockwise direction (as the sun moves).

As you get up, step forward on to your *right* foot, so that you begin stepping round the circle with your *left*.

At each step, your left *heel* must touch the *toe* of your right foot (and vice versa) to maintain continuity.

4. You have now completed the circle and are back at your starting-point. Make sure you don't step outside the circle.

This would oblige you to break it in order to sit down and you would destroy it. Take a step inwards and sit down immediately. Nobody may cross the circle's protective barrier.

Our advice: triple the circle

If there's no one around, go round three times instead of only once. Proceed as above and, after completing the first circle, do two more before taking the step back inside the circle and sitting down. Your circle will be even more powerful.

Fourth method: men only

To attract good luck or to ward off a bad omen, touch your genitals *discreetly* with your right hand.

Fifth method: touch one of your amulets or talismans

This may be a rounded piece of wood (unpolished), an iron key, a nail, or something similar (see **AMULET** and **TALISMAN**).

MARRIAGE

Will you soon be getting married?

Yes!

- If you have recently stumbled going upstairs.
- If a live coal has recently fallen out of the grate at your feet.
- If two teaspoons have been inadvertently placed in one saucer in your presence.

If any of these omens have been vouchsafed you, a marriage is certain in your family – though not necessarily for you.

To find out whom you will marry

Ladies: if you are given a piece of someone else's wedding-cake, put it under your pillow that night and you will dream of the man you are to marry.

Ladies or Men: count seven stars on seven successive nights, and on the eighth day the first person of the opposite sex you shake hands with will be your future husband or wife.

Warning! Except on this occasion it is unlucky to count the stars, and during the ceremony you must be careful to count *only* seven and no more.

How can you make more certain?

Find out what your lover is really thinking: blow a dandelion clock with one breath. The amount of fluff that is left shows how much he or she is thinking about you.

Note You must not cheat or this test is valueless.

To get luck on your side

Don't take the last slice of bread-and-butter from a plate unless it is offered to you. (This applies to *ladies* only.)

Don't stand with the person you are engaged to as godparents to the same child.

Don't go to three funerals in a row – unless you are certain of being able to attend a wedding before a fourth.

Warning to women!

If you are soon to be married, do not allow anyone to call you, even in fun, by your future name. Do not practise your signature before the day, or have anything marked with the new name. If you do so, you may never bear it.

(For omens concerning the wedding-day itself, see under **WEDDING**.)

MINCE PIE

Never refuse a mince pie

A mince pie offered to you by another person is lucky, so *don't refuse it*.

Even if you've already eaten several, if someone offers you another, accept and eat it.

To refuse would bring bad luck for the whole of the coming year.

Our advice

Also be sure to eat *one* mince pie on *each* of the Twelve Days of Christmas. Each one eaten guarantees a month of good luck.

MIRROR

A broken mirror: seven years' bad luck

To break a mirror brings seven years' bad luck.

Avert the omen by:
1. touching wood; or
2. spitting on the pieces; or
3. taking a pinch of salt and throwing it over your left shoulder; or
4. mixing some salt and water together, stirring three times, signing it with the cross, and sprinkling it on the broken pieces.

Reflections can be dangerous

Don't show a baby its reflection in a mirror before it is twelve months old – if you do so, it will never thrive.

Don't look at your reflection in a mirror if there has just been a death in the house – your own or another member of the family's death will follow. After a death, all mirrors should be veiled (see under **GLASS**).

Don't look at your reflection in a mirror if you are a *bride* whilst wearing your wedding-dress – to do so before the ceremony will prevent the marriage.

Don't look at your reflection in a mirror, if you are an *actor*, over someone else's shoulder – this will bring misfortune for the person overlooked.

A fatal omen

If you look in a mirror and see no reflection of yourself – DEATH IS CERTAIN.

MISTLETOE

Mistletoe: a holy plant

Mistletoe is a holy plant – respect it.

Cutting mistletoe

It is *unlucky* to cut mistletoe at any time except Christmas.

It is *extremely unlucky* to cut down a mistletoe-bearing tree, especially an oak. Every kind of misfortune will follow.

Mistletoe wards off thunder

Mistletoe from an oak-tree, if kept in the house, will protect it against thunder and lightning, as well as bringing good luck.

Our advice

Keep your Christmas bunch of mistletoe throughout the year for good luck, replacing it with a new one on the following Christmas Eve.

Mistletoe: bringer of good luck and fertility

To ensure good luck and fertility for the coming year, hang up a Mistletoe Bough or bunch of mistletoe at Christmas.

Hang it in the most frequented part of the house, whether this is the living-room, kitchen or hall.

Everyone who kisses under the mistletoe will ensure the happiness and prosperity of the household for the coming year.

Ladies

If you stand under the mistletoe, you cannot refuse to be kissed by anyone who claims the right to do so.

Not just for lovers

Kissing under the mistletoe is not just for lovers – mistletoe is the plant of peace beneath which, in olden times, even enemies laid down their weapons. So be sure to kiss:

> every member of your family
> friends and relations paying a visit
> neighbours who come to call
> anyone else who will let you!

Set aside your inhibitions

You should kiss members of your own as well as the opposite sex. Men may kiss men, and women women. During this annual ceremony for bringing luck, set aside your usual inhibitions.

Important

This is a ceremony of the **HOME**. A sprig of mistletoe hung up in your office or worn in your buttonhole may produce some pleasant results, but will not in the long term influence your luck.

MONEY

How to attract money

Make your own treasure chest

1. Procure some kind of box: it can be made of wood, metal, china – anything.
2. Place a £5 or a £10 note at the bottom of the box: it will act as a magnet for other notes.
3. Every time you get some money in, whether expected or not, put aside a small sum to increase the nest-egg in your box. As your nest-egg grows, you will find it increasingly easy to make money.

Warning! This money is an offering to your lucky star. The total sum in your treasure chest should never diminish. No coin or note put into the box should ever be taken out. If you fail to observe this strict rule, *your treasure will lose its magnetic qualities.*

Exception If you have, in your little chest, any demonetized coins or notes, take them out and exchange them at the bank. Then, without delay, put the new coins or notes into the box.

To do even better

Use your bank as a magnet.

A. *First stage*

Open a deposit account at the bank (or a Savings Bank account). Your account is bound to earn interest, however small.

B. *Second stage*

Pay a sum of money into this account (this can be anything from one pound to several hundreds, according to your means).

C. *Third stage*

Make out a cheque, drawn in your own name, for an amount equivalent to the sum you have just deposited and place it in your treasure chest.

D. *Fourth stage*

Whenever you receive any money, make it a rule to put a little of it into this deposit/savings account and, at the same time, to place in your chest a cheque for an amount equivalent to your deposit. All the cheques will of course be made out in your own name. Add each year a cheque for an amount equal to the interest paid by the bank or the Savings Bank: this will increase your magnet's power.

For your pocket money

If you have just *found* a bank-note which you are unable to return, fix it to the inside of your pocket with a safety-pin. It too will work like a magnet and other notes of the same value will soon be keeping it company.

Warning! This will only work if there is genuinely no possibility of returning it or handing it in. Luck cannot be coerced by dishonesty.

MOON

The presages of the moon

The moon influences all the vital fluids.

Be on your guard against the moon

Both the full moon ☽ and the new moon ● can cause rages and fits of madness (hence *lunacy* from *luna*, 'moon'). At the full moon, in particular, such an outburst may often result in words or actions which are regretted later on.

Our advice

Never let the moon, especially the full moon, shine on your face when you are in bed. Cover your face with a scarf or a sheet.

For mothers

Children born when there is a full moon will suffer from delicate health.

For those going into hospital

If you are about to go into hospital, you should study the phases of the moon.

1. *The full moon* ☺ can cause haemorrhages, so, except in urgent cases, never undergo an operation at full moon, nor on the day before or after it.
2. *The new moon* ● increases the risk of infection. A surgical incision made at the time of the new moon is more likely to become infected than at any other moment of the lunar month. Try to avoid having operations during this phase of the moon.

NAIL

The nail: a powerful amulet

If you find a nail, luck is smiling on you

If you see a nail on the ground when walking in the street, down the road or anywhere, pick it up and keep it carefully. Luck is smiling on you, for you have just been given one of the most powerful protective **AMULET(S)** there is.

Important This is doubly so if the nail is rusty.

You have a choice

To protect yourself: always keep the nail in your right-hand pocket.
To protect your house: hammer the nail into your kitchen door.

'Once for luck'

Knocking in the nail is *a ritual act* with a prescribed procedure.

1. Point the nail at the spot where you want to knock it in.
2. Strike it with the hammer so that the point of the nail penetrates the wood, at the same time saying, 'Once for luck'.

3. Using *three* strokes of the hammer, knock in the rest of the nail, saying at each successive blow, 'Once for health', 'Once for love', 'Once for money'.

Our advice

For even better protection, hammer the nail, not into the kitchen door itself, but into the frame. Knock it in at eye-level on the side where the lock is, into the wooden surface with which the door is in contact when closed.

If the nail is too big or the doorframe too hard for you to do this, you can fix the nail in vertically, point upwards, at eye-level in the middle of the kitchen door, with two little staples. This is a particularly good solution for very large nails such as rafter nails.

NAPKIN

Don't fold your table-napkin

Use a napkin but . . .

After the first meal eaten in someone else's house, do not fold your table-napkin or you will never eat there again.

Our advice

Leave your napkin crumpled by your plate.

NEW YEAR'S DAY

New Year's Day: make sure of luck for the year

This is a most important day and you should take great care to begin it in the proper manner: it will govern your luck for the rest of the year.

Admitting the First Foot

The 'First Foot' is the first visitor of the New Year to enter a house. He sets the pattern of good or bad luck for the household for the year.

Appoint a luck-bringer

The luckiest First Foot is:

a dark-haired stranger

Rather than rely on the outside chance of such a visit, you may arrange:

- for a friend to act as First Foot to your house;
- for one person to serve as First Foot for several houses or the whole street;
- for an appropriate member of your own family to act as First Foot.

Choosing the First Foot

The First Foot must be:

*a man**

and he should be:

dark haired

He *must not* be:

red-haired
cross-eyed
with eyebrows that meet across his nose

When should the First Foot come?

The First Foot should arrive as soon as the clock has struck midnight.

This is to ensure that no ill-omened person, such as a woman or red-haired man, can arrive before him.

If the First Foot is a member of your own household, be sure to send him outside *before* midnight.

---

* Sorry, ladies – for a woman to do this would be extremely unlucky.   Ed.

Gifts the First Foot should bring

The First Foot should bring with him the following symbolic gifts:

bread = food
coal = warmth
a few coins or some **SALT** = prosperity

Our advice

If you follow these simple rules, you will ensure the luck of your household for the whole of the coming year.

NOISES

Noises: omens of death . . . but not always for you

Spirits are abroad

When you hear noises of unknown origin in the night, it is always a bad omen. In a house which is usually quiet, these creaks or knockings are manifestations of 'rapping' spirits, in Germany known as poltergeists.*

What they tell you

Three raps on the wall of the bedroom or at the head of the bed of a sick person, or any of his relations, is an omen of his death.

A charm against rapping spirits

To prevent disturbance by rapping spirits, hang a large stone with a hole in it at the head of your bed.

---

* It should be pointed out that poltergeist activity is believed by many to be, not the work of spirits, but disturbance produced by children by telekinesis around the age of puberty. Ed.

NUMBER

Your lucky number

Numbers preside over the laws of chance as over most of the laws of nature. Each of us has a lucky number which protects us from ill-fortune.

Calculate your luck

To work it out, you must know that each letter of the alphabet corresponds to a number.

A = 1	H = 8	N = 5	T = 4
B = 2	I = 1	O = 7	U = 6
C = 2	J = 1	P = 8	V = 6
D = 4	K = 2	Q = 1	W = 9
E = 5	L = 3	R = 2	X = 6
F = 8	M = 4	S = 3	Y = 1
G = 3			Z = 7

First step

Write your Christian name and surname in capital letters, then underneath each letter its corresponding number. As an example, let us calculate the lucky number of Victor Hugo.

$$\begin{array}{ccccccccc} V & I & C & T & O & R & H & U & G & O \\ 6 & 1 & 2 & 4 & 7 & 2 & 8 & 6 & 3 & 7 \end{array}$$

Now add together the values of all these letters:

$$6 + 1 + 2 + 4 + 7 + 2 + 8 + 6 + 3 + 7 = 46$$

Second step

Add this number to the year of your birth. (Victor Hugo was born in 1802.)

$$1802 + 46 = 1848$$

Third step

Divide the number obtained by 9, disregard the quotient and keep only the remainder:

$$1848 \div 9 = 205 \text{ (remainder 3)}$$

Note If the remainder equals 0, take it as equal to 9.

99

Fourth step

To the number retained (from 1 to 9), add the number 8.

For Victor Hugo: $3 + 8 = 11$

Fifth step

Finally, to get your lucky number, add together the numbers 1, 2, 3, etc. up to the number obtained (in the fourth step).
For Victor Hugo, we add together all the numbers up to 11.

$$1 + 2 + 3 + 4 + 5 + 6 + 7 + 8 + 9 + 10 + 11 = 66$$

So 66 is Victor Hugo's lucky number.

Sixth step

Write the lucky number you have calculated on a piece of white paper. Fold the paper in four, and put it in a locket or frame, which you should wear round your neck. This number will turn luck in your favour and also protect you from ill fortune.

NUNS

Nuns: ill-omened or bringers of fortune?

Don't look at their backs!

Unlike **CLERGYMEN** and priests, nuns can be either ill-omened or bringers of good fortune.

- To meet one or more nuns is a fortunate omen, *provided that you avoid looking at their backs* when they have passed.
- To see three walking together is especially lucky, again *provided that they are not walking away from you*, so that you see their backs.

Aeroplanes: a special case

For a nun to be among the passengers on an **AEROPLANE** is a bad omen.

Spit for luck

When you see a nun, spit (discreetly) on the ground – this will both avert a bad omen and increase your luck (see **SPITTING**).

NUTMEG

Against rheumatism: the nutmeg

Keep a nutmeg in your pocket

The nutmeg is an effective charm against rheumatism – always carry one in your pocket or you handbag.

Warning! Unlike other **AMULET(S)**, such as nails and keys, it is powerless against the **EVIL EYE**.

OWL

The owl, the bird of misfortune

The owl foretells death or misfortune

- If an owl – particularly a screech-owl – persistently hoots near your house, this is an omen of approaching death.
- If an owl perches on the roof or flies round the house, this is likewise a death-omen.
- If a birth is greeted by an owl hooting, the child will have a difficult life.

Double misfortune

If the owl is heard hooting *by day*, the omen is doubly unfortunate.

Warning! Killing the owl does not avert these omens.

Our advice

An owl's feather, on the contrary, is a powerful charm both for and against evil, so if you find one, keep it carefully.

PARSLEY

Sow parsley on Good Friday

Parsley goes 'nine times to the Devil' before germinating. To prevent this, you must be careful to sow it only on a Good Friday – otherwise there will be a death in the family within a year.

Don't transplant parsley in your garden

It is extremely dangerous *to transplant parsley* at any time: death or misfortune will follow.

It is similarly unlucky *to give parsley roots away*. To do this safely, you must ask the person receiving them to dig them up himself.

An omen for young women

Plant parsley and you can soon expect a child.

PEACH BLOSSOM

Peach blossom: protector of the house

To drive away evil influences

Follow the Chinese custom and hang a branch of peach blossom above the door of your house.

1. Cut a flowering branch about 20 cm long.
2. Hang this branch with a thread of silk, linen or cotton to a nail fixed to the *outside* of the house *above* the door.

Even when withered, it will continue to protect your house.

Our advice

In the right season, try to have a bouquet of peach blossom always on hand. Fix it outside the front door and it will prevent your visitors bringing in any evil spirits they may be afflicted with.

PEA-PODS

Pea-pods: lucky omens

Fresh green peas have an advantage over tinned or frozen ones: they give you a chance of reading the future.

When you are shelling peas

If you find:

- a single pea – this is a lucky omen.
- nine perfect peas – this is even more fortunate.

Note The luck is doubled if this is the first pod you have opened.

Nine peas in a pod cure warts

If you find a pod with nine peas in it, you are in a position to cure someone's warts.

First wrap each pea individually in paper, then bury the wrapped peas. As they shrivel away, so will the warts disappear.

PHOTOGRAPH

Don't pass your photograph around

Most modern sorcerers work from photographs, so if you want to remain as you are:

1. as far as possible avoid being photographed;
2. never hand out photographs of yourself to all and sundry.

Exception If you are on the stage or in films, you hand out photographs every day as part of your work. You may be giving pictures of yourself to people who love and admire you, or to those who hate or are jealous of you, *but this doesn't matter*: the two forces cancel out and you run no risk.

Our advice

If you have to have your picture taken, arrange things so that you are not photographed alone. Put an arm round a friend's waist or shoulders: this will make the photograph useless to those who might wish to harm you.

PICKING UP A GIRL (OR A MAN)

Picking up a girl (or a man): play all your aces

If you have decided to go out and pick up a girl (or a man), here are some signs which foretell possible success or failure.

Favourable encounters

A. Meeting a couple of cats when you are off to pick someone up is extremely favourable. The omen is better still if one of the cats is black and the other white.
B. Meeting a prostitute (male or female) outside a red-light district is a sign of luck. The omen is stronger if you know him or her.

A special case

If you meet a **BLACK CAT**, this is a good omen, especially if it crosses your path.

The first few minutes

If you are having a drink with the person you fancy, and if he or she orders the same drink as you, it is a very favourable sign. This is an even better omen if, instead of saying, 'I feel like a drink', you have mentioned what you are going to drink and received immediate approval, e.g. 'the same for me'.

Men: if your partner accidentally breaks her glass and stains your clothes, take this as an extremely *favourable* omen.

Ladies: be careful! If the man you are after breaks his glass and stains your clothes, this sign is extremely *unfavourable*. This omen is mitigated if the glass breaks without spilling a drop on your clothes.

Favourable omens Wherever you are that evening, power cuts, unexpected storms, and similar events are excellent omens.

A purpose-made talisman

A medallion or a ring covered with strange signs can be used as
104

your 'picking-up talisman' – an important item (see **TALISMAN**).
Give a special power to one of these objects.

1. Take your medallion or your ring, clasp it firmly in both hands and imagine you are holding a powerful magnet which means that you will attract the attention of everyone who looks at you.
2. Imagine at the same time that this talisman will create in everyone an irresistible need to ask you a question.
3. This is the result you have to achieve.

Once the question has been asked, you have fate on your side and you have also made the most significant moment easier, that is to say, the moment of making contact.

Wear this talisman so that everyone can see it

It should excite curiosity (unlike all other talismans).

Favourable words

Use all the words which are apt to arouse emotion: 'charm', 'beauty', 'intelligence', 'seductive', and so forth. All these words are favourable if used solely in speaking of your partner; if used otherwise, they will turn against you.

Special scent for pick-up artists

Your only scent should be a musk-based one.

Improve it! Put some scent in the palms of your hands and run them slowly over your whole body, imagining the success you are going to have tonight. This action will change your skin secretions which will then give off a particular odour. This odour will mingle with the scent and will give it more 'body' and a powerful sensual attraction.

Warning! You have to choose between the pleasure of picking someone up and of just shooting a line, so never say, e.g., 'He/she is crazy about me.' This would unfailingly attract bad luck.

Never talk about your failures

In recounting one of your failures, you increase its significance. Next time there would be two factors for failure, as two persons (rather than one) would have doubts about whether you could make it.

105

Unfavourable encounters

When setting out to pick someone up, it is unlucky to meet:

a priest
a member of any sect which imposes sexual taboos
a **CLERGYMAN**, monk or **NUN**

All these figures are unfavourable in these circumstances. This omen is more serious if you know any of them well.

Avert the omen, ladies, by touching a rusty **NAIL** or iron **KEY**.

Men: you have a natural advantage here; you can just break the spell by discreetly touching your genitals. This custom is very widespread in Italy and it is the Romans (world-famous pick-up artists) who have most frequent recourse to it (as sudden encounters with priests and nuns are very common in their city).

Our advice

Study the methods we have just suggested carefully. Compare your own experience: you will know that everything is in order when you are regularly picked up.

Don't forget! The best way of picking up someone is to be picked up oneself.

PIN

Pins: both harm and protect

Because they are sharp and made of steel, pins can both harm you and protect you (see also **AXE**, **KNIFE**, **SCISSORS**). They are therefore both lucky and unlucky, according to circumstance.

Finding a pin

If you are out walking or shopping, and find a pin on the ground, this is a lucky omen provided that:

1. you pick it up immediately;
2. its point is away from you.

106

But, if its point is *towards* you, leave it strictly alone – to pick it up would be to 'pick up sorrow'.

Don't give or lend pins

1. It is unlucky to give pins as a gift to a friend – they will pierce your friendship (cf. **SCISSORS**).

Exception The omen is averted if the friend gives you something – a small coin for example – in return.

2. It is unlucky also to lend pins.

Exception The omen is averted if you do not hand them over, but invite the borrower to help himself.

Warning! In both cases, it is unlucky to say 'thank you' for the pins.

Don't take pins on board ship

Pins are extremely ill-omened objects to have on board a ship as they may cause the vessel to leak or, if it is a fishing-boat, tear the nets.

An omen for dressmakers

If, when you are fitting a garment on a customer, you accidentally pin it to his or her old clothes, count the number of pins you have used in doing so – this will tell you the number of years until your marriage.

Pins as an offering

Pins (not coins, as people seem to think) are the luckiest offering to make at wishing and healing wells.

Note The pin should first be bent or twisted to 'kill' it, i.e. render it harmless.

Pins to protect your house

Pins can be used to protect your house against malign influences.

1. Stick a pin into the doorpost (see also **KNIFE**).
2. Fill a bottle with pins and keep it on the hearth, or better still, in old houses, under the hearthstone.

Note The pins must be *bent* for the reason given above.

PLATE

Broken plates: a bad omen

If a bride breaks a plate at her wedding reception, this is a bad omen: her marriage will be unhappy.

Breakages come in threes

If you accidentally break a plate or other piece of china, be certain that two more breakages will follow.

To render this omen harmless

In order to make sure that nothing you treasure is broken, immediately *fulfil the omen* by smashing two more things of little value or else pieces of the object already broken. That way you will sustain no serious loss.

PLAYING CARDS

Have you got a pack of cards? Its fate is bound up with your own

Don't tempt fate

1. If you follow a dangerous occupation (miner, seaman, pilot, etc.) don't take your pack of cards with you: this would bring you bad luck.
2. A tip for burglars: in the underworld, it's common knowledge that when you burgle a house or a flat, you don't steal packs of cards or else you'll get caught.

Our advice: to avoid your cards bringing you bad luck on a journey

If you *have* to travel with your cards, just wrap the pack in a violet silk square before putting it in your pocket.

Don't throw cards away

Don't throw a pack of cards into the dustbin, even an old pack. To throw the cards away is to throw away luck.

If you have to get rid of an old pack of cards, you must destroy them by fire, and not before buying a new pack to replace them.

While the old pack is burning, take the new one out of its case and wave it three times in the smoke.

This advice applies to any pack of cards, including those used for fortune telling (such as Tarot packs).

Treat your packs of cards with respect

● If you have used a pack of cards to tell fortunes, don't use it for a game.

● If you have, on the other hand, used a pack for card-games, do not use it for fortune telling.

The two types of use are incompatible.

Cards in the house

Put away the cards used for *playing* in a room to which all visitors have access – the entrance-hall or the living-room will do perfectly well. Put them in a small box and place it on a table.

But put the cards you use for *divination* in a room to which strangers do not have access and in a place known only to you.

Our advice

Before putting away any pack of cards, always wrap it in a violet silk square.

For gamblers: one card brings you luck

If you are an inveterate gambler, be sure to watch the cards. Whenever you win a game, you will always have been dealt one particular card on the first deal. This is your lucky card. Everybody has one and it's up to you to discover yours. This lucky card never appears on the first deal when you're losing.

Once you have discovered this lucky card, touch it with the index finger of your left hand before each game and you will increase your chances of winning.

Important Don't be surprised if your lucky card is one that is usually reckoned to be ill-omened. In this particular case, it works for *you* and for *your* luck at play – and that's all.

Our advice: touch a high card

If you haven't succeeded in discovering which your lucky card is, or if you haven't managed to touch it before the game starts, touch any high card – an ace, for example.

For good luck, take these precautions

A. When you cut, always use the left hand.
B. When you pick up a trick, always use the right hand.
C. When you win, pick up your winnings without counting them. Not to count your winnings gives you an additional chance of winning the next game – and this is true even if you are playing at home with your family for matchsticks.
D. If you want to win, sit on your handkerchief or your jacket pocket.
E. Before going out to play cards, stick a pin in the hem of your dress or trousers.

Are you going to lose? How to find out

Examine the hand you have been dealt.

In all games, a run of Spades brings bad luck for that game. If you are dealt the four of Clubs on the first deal, you will not have any luck either.

In poker, on the first deal, two pairs, Aces and eights, bring bad luck.

When you are dealing, a card falling face upwards is always a bad omen. Here, Spades and Clubs are worse than Hearts or Diamonds. If you have first deal and deal yourself the nine of Diamonds, you will lose the game through some careless mistake.

Our advice: only one way to break the spell

Get up, pick up your chair and turn round with it three times. Spit under it before recommencing play.

To make your games of Patience come out: make up your own pack

Once made up, this pack will be a real **TALISMAN**.

110

1. Buy a number of identical packs of cards (same make, size and colour). You need at least ten identical packs.
2. Number the cases of these packs from 1 to 10 in order to identify them.
3. Take pack No 1 and set out a game of Patience. If it comes out, start again, once, twice, etc.
4. Once a card is badly placed and stops you getting the game out, take this card, throw it into a box put aside for this purpose and replace it in your stock with an identical card from pack No 2 (make a note on the case of this pack that you have taken out this card). Continue to play, each time replacing in your stock the card which 'blocks' you with the identical card taken from one of the nine packs you have in reserve. You will soon have a pack which will enable you to make your game of Patience come out pretty nearly every time. Carry this remarkable pack about with you: it's a lucky charm.

Note This game is never finished. Every blocking card has to be eliminated as explained above. Keep what is left of the ten packs, and always have a new pack in reserve, but throw any cards you have eliminated on to a brushwood fire, kindled out in the open, and walk away without turning round. Your bad luck goes up in smoke with them.

Your cards foretell the future

Whenever a card happens to catch your eye, it's a sign of fate. Pay heed to the warning:

- if you find a card in the street or while doing the housework;
- if one of the cards meant for you turns over on the table during the deal;
- if, when picking up cards lying on the table, you drop a card or a card turns over.

Spades or Swords foretell difficulties

Ace: sign of mourning or imminent catastrophe. Possibly separation or break-up.
King: conflict with the law or lawsuit.
Queen: slander or libel concerning you.
Knave: difficulties or dispute with a child, a grandchild or a subordinate.
Ten: tells you of a set-back to your current projects or of serious difficulties.
Nine: delay in all areas.

Eight: you are going to get some bad news.
Seven: disappointment, vexation.

Diamonds or Batons

Ace: a letter or an important piece of news is delayed.
King: treachery or a broken promise.
Queen: indiscretions are going to put you in a difficult situation.
Knave: bad news or an unpleasant letter.
Ten: short trip, compulsory move.
Nine: the arrival of money you are expecting will be delayed.
Eight: obstacles and difficulties in current negotiations but these will not prevent your success. The Eight merely urges you to be careful.
Seven: small unexpected windfall or you will save on some small anticipated expenditure.

Clubs or Coins

Ace: foretells a success in social or professional life.
King: shrewd advice or support of a man of experience or a businessman.
Queen: people speak well of you and this is going to be useful.
Knave: bad news or an unpleasant letter.
Ten: your financial situation will improve or you will be getting some money.
Nine: a valuable present, a gift of money or an unexpected income.
Eight: financial profits or a successful business deal concluded.
Seven: proposal for a business deal or a partnership. It comes from an irresponsible person. *Refuse.* He's dreaming!

Hearts or Cups

Ace: harmony at home, in the family or circle of friends (either continuing or recommencing). End of a domestic conflict.
King: for the moment, you are protected from anxieties and misfortunes.
Queen: love will come your way.
Knave: a new friendship.
Ten: emotional satisfaction provided by husband, wife, lover, child or grandparents.
Nine: joy or triumph in some sphere or other.
Eight: a party or the celebration of a success.
Seven: tenderness in the days to come or consolation if you are unhappy. Moral support.

112

For all suits: the low cards

The Two, Three, Four or Five: when accidentally dropped from a pack, only give a vague indication of what fate may have in store.

Spades: unexpected troubles.
Diamonds: material obstacles.
Clubs: a sign of luck.
Hearts: unexpected satisfaction.

Warning! Don't use these omens to read your fortune. The interpretations given here only apply when a card turns up fortuitously.

Our advice

To ward off the bad omens of 'windfall' cards, counter them by carrying the 'opposing' card on your person for twenty-eight days (one lunar month): Hearts v. Spades (Cups v. Swords), Clubs v. Diamonds (Coins v. Batons), Kings v. Kings, Queens v. Queens, etc.

Example The Ace of Spades has been dropped:
1. Put the Ace of Hearts in your wallet or your pocket. You can even make a sachet and wear it round your neck. The important thing is not to forget to carry or wear it for the next twenty-eight days.
2. Take the rest of the pack, including the card of ill-omen, and burn it.
3. When the twenty-eight days during which you have carried or worn the beneficent card are up, put it on a small plate with a drop of spirits and burn it: if nothing predicted by the ill-omened card has happened to you, you have broken the spell.

Stained or damaged cards: these accidents have a meaning!

If you stain or tear a card while playing Patience, telling your own fortune or someone else's, or doing the housework, this is a warning that the omen borne by that particular card will be reversed.

Note that the position of the stain indicates the seriousness of the omen; that a torn *Heart* or *Club* is always *ill-omened*, and that a torn *Spade* or *Diamond* is always *favourable*.

You accidentally stain an Ace of Hearts (or Cups)

• If the stain is in a corner or on the side of the card, a threat hovers over the harmony of your home (as the Ace of Hearts foretells).

- If the stain covers the central image of the Heart (or Cup), this is the presage of a quarrel or of the break-up of the home.

You accidentally tear an Ace of Hearts (or Cups)

- If only the corner is torn or the tear is not a complete one and the card is still in one piece: a threat hovers over you both.
- If the card is torn in two more or less equal pieces, this means the break-up of the home.

You stain or tear an Ace of Spades (or Swords)

- If the stain is in the corner or on the side of the card, or the card is not torn through or just a corner is torn, because this card as a rule foretells mourning, catastrophes or quarrels, the stain or tear forecasts that these misfortunes will be avoided. In general, the stained Ace of Spades foretells trouble for those who, through their position or their intentions, are doing you harm in one way or another.
- If the stain covers the central image of the Spade (or Sword), this means the death of an enemy or of someone who, through his position or his intentions, is impeding your success in society or has an interest in destroying your home.

You stain or tear a Knave of Clubs

- If the stain is in the corner or on the side of the card, or the card is not torn through or just a corner is torn, the friend who is coming to your assistance has problems and will not be able to do so.
- If the stain is on the picture of the Knave or the card is torn in two, the friend who was coming to your assistance will be forced to betray you.

You stain or tear a Knave of Diamonds

- If the stain is in the corner or on the side of the card, or the tear is incomplete or only a corner of the card is torn, the letter or the bad news is delayed – the delay may be considerable.
- If the stain is on the picture of the Knave or the card is torn in two, the bad news or the unpleasant letter predicted will never reach you.

Our advice

To avert the omens from stained or torn cards, follow this procedure, taking as our example the Ace of Hearts.

1. Stain or tear the Ace of *Spades*, and put it in your wallet or your pocket. The important thing is not to forget to wear it for the next twenty-eight days.
2. Take the rest of the pack, including the stained or torn Ace of *Hearts* and burn it.
3. When the twenty-eight days during which you have carried the 'opposing' card are up, put it on a small plate with a few drops of spirits and burn it: if nothing this unlucky card foretold for you has happened, you have averted the omen.

PRECIOUS STONES

Precious stones: presages and properties

1. Agate

Worn as a pendant, it will protect you from the **EVIL EYE**.

If you have an agate ring, wear it on the little finger of your right hand, unless you wish to enhance your *eloquence*, in which case wear it on the little finger of your left hand.

2. Loadstone

Worn as a pendant, it will protect you from various pains and also increase your natural luck.

3. Amber

Worn as a necklace it will help you keep calm and will ward off the **EVIL EYE**.

4. Amethyst

Whether you wear it as a ring or a pendant, or keep it in your pocket, it will not only encourage temperance, but actively protect you from the effects of alcohol, improve your memory and ward off bad dreams.

5. Coral

Worn as a necklace or other form of jewellery, it will protect you

115

from ill fortune, also from haemorrhages and skin diseases. (See **AMULET** and **BABY**).

6. Diamond

As well as being the (commercial) symbol of lasting love, it will bring you luck in financial matters. Mounted in a silver ring and worn on the ring-finger of the left hand, it will help you sleep.

7. Emerald

Promotes second sight and intuition.

8. Garnet

Worn on your person, it stimulates wit and makes you appear more brilliant than you are.

Warning! Don't buy a garnet or let anyone give you one. Troubles will not be long in coming.

9. Jade

Whether worn as a jewel or not, it's a real **TALISMAN**, a good-luck charm for you and also your home.

10. Jasper

Worn either in a ring or a brooch, on the *left* side of your body, it will both help and protect you.

11. Magnetite

Men only: worn on your person, it will increase your strength and virility.

12. Opal

ALWAYS UNLUCKY!

Exception The black opal, a powerful **TALISMAN**.

13. Ruby

Worn as a ring or a pendant, it protects from diseases of the blood and circulation. Wear it to increase your physical vigour, too.

14. Sapphire

Worn as a pendant, on a white metal chain, it will soothe aching eyes if held to the forehead.

15. Turquoise

Wear it as a pendant on your solar plexus or as a brooch (in the same place).

Your pendant should always hang on a gold chain; your brooch should be mounted on gold.

If you wear your turquoise as a ring, it should be worn on the forefinger of the right hand. Your ring should, of course, be a gold one.

PREGNANCY

Pregnancy: avoid harming your child

What happens to you, happens to your child

Madam: if you are pregnant, remember that everything that happens to you also happens to your child. If something frightens you, your baby may be born with a birthmark of the same shape as whatever frightened you – whether animal, reptile or bird.

Our advice

If your baby is born with a birthmark, try the powerful effects of **SPITTLE**. You must:

1. Lick the birthmark *every morning* for 9 or 21 mornings, beginning as soon as possible after the child is born.
2. Lick the birthmark *all over* – this is important.
3. Do this *fasting*, i.e. before you have had anything to eat or drink.

Avoid hares

If you see a hare, you risk your child being born with a hare-lip. Usually it is possible to avoid places where hares are known to congregate. But if you *do* accidentally see a hare, **avert the omen**

117

by stopping as soon as you see it, and making three small tears in your clothes.

Avoid places where cyclamen grow

If you have a woodland garden where cyclamen have been naturalized, or if you go on holiday to a Mediterranean country such as Greece, be careful that you do not tread on a cyclamen: this could cause a *miscarriage*.

Note Indoor and greenhouse cyclamen are, in the normal course of things, no danger to you.

Our advice: broaden your mind

During your pregnancy, get down to some serious reading. Take advantage of the time to broaden your mind. Your child will be the more intelligent.

Don't tempt fate!

Don't bring a new pram or a new cot into your house before the child is born. This would bring him bad luck.

PRESENT

Signs that a present is on its way

You are going to receive a present

1. If a white spot appears on your thumb-nail (see **FINGER**).
2. If you sneeze before breakfast and/or on Thursday (see **SNEEZING**).

PULLOVER

The pullover: a lucky garment

A good habit

When you put on a pullover, make sure you put your arms into the sleeves before pulling it over your head. This protects you from *drowning*. Note that putting on a pullover head first doesn't mean you'll actually meet your death by drowning. It merely deprives you of the protection provided by this good habit.

Mending your pullover

If there's a hole in your pullover, be sure to mend it with a woollen thread the same colour or, failing that, a lighter shade. *Never use a thread that is darker than the pullover* – this will bring you bad luck.

RED RIBBON

Red ribbon: a protection for little girls

Red wards off malign influences

Red is a lucky colour for little girls. Tie a red ribbon in your daughter's hair and it will defend her against malign influences until she reaches the age of puberty.

ROPE

Rope: protects you from lumbago

Everyone who has a sedentary job or who does a lot of heavy work is liable to suffer from the unpleasant affliction known as lumbago.

119

Our advice

If you have to do a sedentary job, you can avoid the curse of lumbago by replacing your belt with a length of hempen rope.

Hempen rope worn as a belt is a very effective charm against this particular misfortune.*

SALT

Salt protects you from bad luck

Protect yourself

When you are about to undertake anything important, carry a small handful of salt in your pocket to protect yourself from bad luck. (See especially **MARRIAGE**.)

Our advice

For this and all the following rituals, we advise you to buy some coarse sea salt from a health shop or a large store.

Protect your house

See **HOUSE** and **NEW YEAR'S DAY**.

For Baby

So that he lacks for nothing in later life, a minute pinch of salt and one of sugar should be put into your baby's mouth when he makes his first visit to another house, or else salt should be included among his presents (see **BABY**).

It is unlucky

- To pass anyone the salt at table – help him to salt and you 'help him to sorrow'.

* This cure is given without alteration for the benefit of lumbago-sufferers, but be warned that it may not work. Up to this century in Britain hempen rope was a popular cure – chiefly for headaches – but it had to be *hangman's rope*.   Ed.

- To upset a salt-cellar between friends – quarrels will ensue.
- To spill salt – to avert the bad luck, take a pinch of the spilt salt and throw it over your left shoulder. Do this three times.
- To borrow salt.

Exception If this is done by the original owner. It is even unluckier to return salt than to borrow it, and the only safe way it can be done is for the person who lent it to ask to 'borrow' it back.

Use salt to change your luck

1. Mix a handful of sea salt with water.
2. Stir it three times.
3. Make the sign of the cross over it.

Sprinkle this solution over any unlucky thing and it will remove the bad luck.

SCISSORS

Scissors cut the thread of life

Beware of dropping scissors!

If you have just dropped a pair of scissors accidentally, beware: death is on the watch.

- If they fall *points downwards*, this means a death in the house or in the immediate neighbourhood.
- If a *dressmaker* drops her scissors, this is a sign that she may soon expect more work – but probably for clothes to be worn at funerals.

Warning! Don't pick the scissors up yourself. Ask someone else to pick them up for you, as to do so yourself would be doubly unlucky. Whoever does this service for you will incur no ill luck, provided that he or she *closes the scissors before picking them up*.

Never give scissors as a gift

Never give scissors as a gift to a friend without receiving a small coin from them in 'payment'. Otherwise your friendship will be cut.

Protect your house

- Open a pair of scissors to form a cross, and lay them on the threshold of your house; or,
- Close a pair of scissors and thrust them into the doorpost. Either will serve to keep your house from harm.

SELLING

Sell more – sell better

Tips for those who work in selling

A. Dress in a harmony of greys.
B. Wear a cinnamon-based toilet water.
C. Keep a small glass tube filled with mercury in your left-hand pocket or your handbag.

Take care! The tube should be sealed with wax.

Our advice

If you're unable to get a glass tube with mercury in it, put a clinical thermometer in your pocket: it can be left in its case.

If you work in a market or a shop

To ensure a good day's trading, spit on the coin you receive in payment for the first purchase of the day. If the customer pays in notes or by cheque, don't spit. Wait for the first coin.

SEVEN

Seven: a prophetic number

Seven days, seven months, seven years

The cycle of life goes in sevens and the end of each of these periods always brings a change.

122

After seven years: a new person

Because the cycle of human life runs in seven-year spans, each person is totally renewed every seven years.

So do not despair: a child who is difficult at seven, may be a paragon at fourteen, likewise the problems of fourteen vanish at twenty-one.

SEXUALITY

Sexuality: how to be irresistible

Some practical instructions

Bewitch her in the restaurant

Men: if you have invited the woman you desire to a restaurant, wait until the coffee comes round, then discreetly take a lump of sugar and excuse yourself for a few moments. Disappear, warm the sugar between your hands and moisten it slightly with your saliva. Contrive to slip this sugar lump into your companion's coffee: she will be unable to resist your charm.

Ladies: naturally, you can make use of this method too.

If she has given you a date but . . .

If you are uncertain of her feelings towards you, before leaving your house, take a piece of red cloth; shut yourself in a dark room and draw a heart on it, while concentrating on her image for at least ten minutes. Then roll the cloth into a ball and put it under your left armpit. Keep it there throughout your rendezvous. This method is very effective.

Ladies: this also works for you.

Are you shy, sir?

If she seems susceptible to your charms but you dare not pronounce the words or make a decisive move:

1. stand in front of a mirror and look steadily at the reflection of the bridge of your nose (your expression should be firm and imperious, like a conqueror's);
2. describe, in a low voice, the caresses you are going to lavish on your beloved, the embraces you are going to enjoy; and

123

3. when you meet her, adopt the expression you had in front of the mirror – she will melt into your arms.

Warning! Ladies, this method will get you nowhere – don't try it.

If he or she deserts you, use the magic of love

Don't wait until the situation gets worse: use this effective way of winning your loved one back.

The apple of love

1. Go into the orchard one morning before sunrise and pick the nicest apple you can see. (If you live in a town, you can buy your apple in a shop but the spell will be less effective.)
2. Take a piece of white paper about 5 cm wide and write on it with a few drops of your blood:
    a) your surname and Christian name;
    b) the surname and Christian name of your beloved.
3. On another piece of paper of the same size, write the word 'SHEUA'.
4. Place the two pieces of paper face to face.
5. Roll them together.
6. Tie this roll with three of your hairs and three of your beloved's hairs.
7. Cut the apple in two, take out the pips and put the paper in the space thus formed.
8. Join the two halves of the apple with some *rusty* nails (see under **NAIL**).
9. Dry the apple in the oven until there is no trace of moisture left.
10. When it's really dry, wrap your apple in laurel leaves and myrtle leaves. (If you can't find any myrtle, just use laurel.)
11. Put the apple underneath the bed of the person concerned. All you need to do now is wait for your stratagem to work – it shouldn't take long.

NB This will work for both sexes.

Long-distance seduction

If you love a man who takes no interest in you: make him look at you

1. Take a bath.
2. Scent yourself.
3. Make yourself as erotic as possible.
4. Stretch out in a quiet, dark spot.

5. Close your eyes and relax completely.

6. Think of the man you love. Try to picture his face and body in the greatest detail. See him just as if he were in front of you.

7. Once you have successfully conjured up his image, 'dissolve' into him. Mingle his image with yours.

8. Carry out this ritual as often as possible. He will not be long in showing an interest in you.

Note Men can also carry out this ritual.

Men only: an aphrodisiac

If you're afraid you won't be up to it this evening, put a handful of sticks of celery in about half a litre of cold water and bring it to the boil. Continue boiling until the celery is pulpy. This concoction tastes horrible – *but what superb results*!

Our advice

These days, a lot of magazines suggest so-called 'occult' techniques for arousing desire. Most often, these involve concentrating in front of the photo of the person you want, while swearing that he or she wants to make love to *you*. Some even go so far as to advise you to masturbate in front of the photo. Such techniques are generally ineffective: what they principally do is make the *person who practises them* mad with desire. We are not saying that they are bad, but they should be practised only by those rare experts who have undergone special physical, mental and spiritual training, a long and arduous course under the guidance of a master in that particular discipline.

SHIP

Don't unleash the fury of the sea

Before even going on board, it is necessary to observe certain rules, otherwise you risk unleashing the fury of the seas against you or your ship.

How to board

All the passengers and members of the crew must step on board with *the right foot first*. This is most important.

Undesirable passengers

A. A woman
B. A clergyman.

Exception If he or she is a member of the crew, the omen is invalid.

Never take these on board

1. Rabbits – alive or dead. They are very unlucky.
2. Eggs – but this only applies *after sunset*. To take them on board at any other time of the day is perfectly harmless.

Do take this on board

A black cat on board is a very lucky sign – it will serve as a mascot (see further under **BLACK CAT**).

What you must never say

Certain words which are perfectly harmless elsewhere must never be pronounced on a ship or even a sailing-boat. These are the words 'cat', 'dog', 'hare', 'pig', 'rabbit' and 'rat'; 'egg', 'salt'; 'knife'; and any mention of drowning – 'drown', 'drowning', 'drowned'.

Averting the omen The omen can be averted if, as soon as the taboo word has been spoken, the speaker and all those who have heard it immediately touch 'cold iron'.

Whistling on board a ship

Normally *never whistle on board a ship*. This is extremely ill-omened – it will raise a storm (see further under **WHISTLING**).

Exception The only appropriate time to whistle on board a ship is when you are on a sailing boat and it is becalmed. But do so only very softly – just enough to raise a wind, not create a tempest.

Before weighing anchor for the first time: christen the ship

At the launching of a ship, omit the ceremony of breaking a bottle of champagne on the bows at your peril. If you withhold this
126

sacrifice to the sea, you will pay the price in some other way, perhaps with a human life.

Note At the launching, if the person who is christening the ship doesn't succeed first time in smashing the champagne bottle, this is a bad omen. The ship will run into trouble of every kind.

Our advice

Certain small boats are not fitted to undergo the ceremony with the champagne bottle, their hulls being too fragile. In this case, the boat should be christened by simply opening the bottle of champagne and sprinkling the contents on the stem-post. The champagne which runs off the stem and into the sea is an offering to the gods of the sea – their anger will be appeased.

Don't give a ship a new name

Never give a ship or even a small boat a new name. If you have just bought a boat from her owner, take her with her old name – it's part of her. *Do not re-christen her:* this would be tempting fate.

Our advice

Be sure to keep your boat's original name. Don't give your boat or a ship, even for the first time, a name ending in the letter *a*: this would be disastrous. Remember the *Lusitania*!

Don't lend equipment to another ship

Don't lend anything belonging to your ship or boat to another vessel, or your luck will go with it.

Exception If it is absolutely necessary that something be lent to another ship, first ritually 'kill' the object you must lend. The tiniest scratch or dent is enough to avert the misfortune.

Fatal signs: don't sail!

- If on the way to the ship your path has been crossed by a hare, a pig or a rabbit – turn back.
- If a broom or bucket has been lost overboard.
- If anything has been stolen from your ship – part of her luck will have gone with it.

127

- If someone points at the ship as she is going out to sea – ill luck will befall all those aboard her and she will probably not return.
- If a table-glass has suddenly started to ring of its own accord in your home or a restaurant – shipwreck! (See **GLASS**.)
- If the rats have left the ship just before she gets under way – she will be wrecked on the trip. DON'T SAIL!

Our advice

Rats may seem to you unpleasant little creatures, but their presence on board a ship is an excellent omen for sailors.

On a cruise: fate tolls the knell

If someone should die on board during a cruise, whether because of accident or illness, *his body belongs to the sea* and should be buried at sea, wrapped in a shroud. It is very ill-omened to bring the body back to land.

Our advice

Circumstances or the law may oblige you to do otherwise.

Avert the omen on the day of the burial by throwing into the sea a wreath with the name of the deceased on its ribbon and a lighted candle fixed on it.

This rite is appropriate for the West and for Westerners, who are buried with flowers.

Other sailors, other customs: let us respect them

If the dead person is being buried according to an Eastern rite, instead of a wreath, a small boat or raft must be made on which offerings are placed identical to those which would be placed on a tomb. With these offerings goes a lighted candle.

Our advice

In the East, offerings of food, drink and incense should replace the wreaths and flowers used in the West.

To protect your boat

Boats no longer have figureheads. This is a pity, as they had both a protective and a decorative function. They were genuine **AMULET(S)**.

What you can do instead

To replace the figurehead, you can paint on the boat's bows two eyes representing the 'Eye of Horus'. This hieroglyphic is designed to keep away evil spirits. The eyes are painted on either side of the stem post.

Our advice

The fashion for multi-hull sailing boats somewhat complicates this business of protecting your boat.

1. *Catamarans:* you must protect both hulls by painting a pair of eyes on each.
2. *Trimarans:* if the central hull is longer than the outriggers, it is the only one that needs protecting. But if all three hulls are the same length, you must give each a pair of eyes. All six eyes must be the same size and colour – use a stencil.

To ensure good luck at sea

1. Drive a knife into the mast of the ship or boat (see under **KNIFE**).
2. If you are a sailor, wear a sprig of hazel under your cap.
3. Carry a lump of **COAL** that has 'come from the sea', i.e. fallen off a ship and been washed ashore.

SHIT

Shit (stepping in it)

If you step in some (usually dog-) shit, this will bring you luck but only under two conditions:

- it must be *with your left foot*;
- it must be by *accident*.

Warning! It's no use stepping in it on purpose to attract good luck. This won't work.

SHOELACES

Your shoelaces tell you about the present

If you find a knot in your shoelaces, rejoice: luck is on your side. You will be fortunate for the rest of the day.

Our advice

Use your luck. Begin some new enterprise – it is sure to succeed.

SHOES

Shoes: they have some surprises in store for you!

A shoe gives you warning

Bad luck will certainly pursue you:

- if you accidentally put your right foot into your left shoe;
- if you put your left shoe on first whilst dressing;
- if you leave your shoes crossed on the floor at night.

130

Our advice

Avoid incurring misfortune in this fashion by placing your shoes in the shape of a T.

Special cases

- If you are a *jockey*: it is unlucky for you to place your boots on the floor before a race. Make sure that they are left where you usually keep them, until you are ready to put them on.
- If you are a *miner*: it is a very bad omen to dream of cracked or damaged shoes.
- If you are a *fisherman*: your seaboots should never be brought to you over someone's shoulder. They must be tucked under the arm, otherwise this is a very bad omen.
- If you are an *actor*: when you take your shoes off in your dressing-room, don't put them on a chair – and don't let anyone else do so either – for this ensures bad luck.

Squeaking shoes

Shoes that squeak are a sign that a cobbler has not been paid. But if an *actor's* shoes squeak as he makes his first entrance, he will have an appreciative audience (see under **THEATRE**).

Putting shoes on the table

Don't put your shoes on a **TABLE**, especially if they are new: this foretells a quarrel or even death.

Exception If a woman does this, it foretells the birth of a child within the year, her own or someone else's in the family.

Judging character by shoes

The way in which shoes wear is a sign of character. Watch out for shoes mended in certain places.

At the toe – the owner will suffer misfortune.
Along the side – the owner (female) will be a bride.
On the sole – the owner is a spendthrift.
On the heel – the owner is a miser.

131

The shoe in business

Crooks, swindlers and other unscrupulous persons are 'foot-proud', i.e. they very frequently wear showy and expensive shoes.

What is more, the shoes worn by these people seem to stay miraculously free from all traces of dirt or mud, dents or even dust.

If you take a walk with someone and his shoes get dirty less quickly than yours, DON'T TRUST HIM.

On the other hand, if his shoes seem to attract the mud and if they get dirty quicker than yours, your relationship with him will be a happy one.

Our advice

In business, never trust people who wear expensive shoes with cheap clothes. On the other hand, when your companion's clothes are of better quality than his shoes, you are probably dealing with an honest man. He is probably even rather green where business is concerned.

A good tip

If you suffer from cramp or rheumatism, leave your shoes on the floor at night *with their soles uppermost*. With luck, you'll find that your symptoms disappear.

Throw shoes for good luck

A.   After a newly married couple leaving for their honeymoon. It is doubly lucky if you manage to hit one of them – but be careful! The cautious may tie the shoes to the back of the bridal car.
B.   After anyone – not just newly-weds – setting out on a journey.
C   After someone going off to a new job.
D.   After a ship leaving harbour.

Important In all these cases, you are throwing luck to the person or ship by imparting to them a little of the life-essence of the shoes' wearer. Therefore *the shoes must be old*, whether they are yours or someone else's, and never new.

Shoes foretell the future

A bride departing on her honeymoon should stand at the head of the stairs and throw her right shoe (the one she was married in) among the unmarried wedding-guests. The person who catches it will be the next one to marry.

SHOOTING

Beware of inauspicious encounters

If, before you have fired a single shot, you meet:

    a clergyman
    a pregnant woman

cross your fingers immediately or go back home. You risk either returning with an empty bag or being the victim of an accident.

Our advice: for those who want to shoot a particular type of game

A. Take 1) a large sheet of paper,
          2) a thick pencil or new felt-tip pen.
B. Very carefully draw the type of game you want to shoot.
C. Hang the sheet of paper up as a target and shoot at your drawing.

New Year's Eve

On New Year's Eve, fire a shot* into the air at midnight to see the Old Year out and the New Year in. This will bring you good luck for the twelve months to come.

SHOW-DOWN

For a show-down: strict rules

If you decide to have a show-down, there are definite rules you must observe in order to have the best chances of success.

* Your cartridge doesn't have to contain shot: ask your gunsmith for a blank.

Choose a favourable time

Unless you have been asked to a meeting, don't have any show-downs between the full moon and the new moon. Before fixing up the meeting, consult your almanac or your calendar.

The full moon is represented thus: ☺

The new moon thus: ●

Avoid green

Don't wear anything green. Green is an unfavourable colour for everything to do with business, administration and the professions. To wear it is to court failure.

Don't be shy

Never sit with your back to the door when you are in the office of the person you have come to see. If the chair you are offered has its back to the door, move it a quarter-turn before sitting down.

Never allow yourself to be facing the window. Seat yourself at an angle or alongside it. (Move your chair a quarter or an eighth of a turn.)

Don't let yourself be intimidated

Don't hesitate *to stand up* to express your views if you see that the other person's chair is higher than yours. Follow these rules and most of the show-downs you're involved in will be successful (provided your proposals are realistic). Your point of view will carry the day.

Our advice

When you speak, look the other person straight in the eye. When he speaks, keep your eyes on a level with his stomach.

SHROVE TUESDAY

Shrove Tuesday: ensure your luck for the year

Tossing the pancake

On Shrove Tuesday, make some pancakes and toss them, each person tossing his or her own. You *must* eat the pancake you have tossed, however disastrous, or it will bring you no luck.

Make pancakes and learn the future

Single girls still living at home can use their Shrove Tuesday pancakes to learn the future.

What to do

If you live on a farm or just keep a few chickens:

1. give the first pancake made to the cock;
2. count the number of hens that come to help him eat it.

This will be the number of months or years that must pass before you will get married.

Warning! Do not make a second pancake before the cock has been given the first, or the omen will be worthless.

SICKLE

The sickle protects your house

A charm against lightning

Like other implements made of iron and steel, the sickle can be a strong protection for your house (see **AXE**, **KNIFE**, **SCISSORS**, **SPADE**). In particular it can be used as a charm against lightning.

How to use the sickle

If you have a house with a chimney, position the sickle on its *north* face so that:

135

1. the crescent of the sickle opens to the *east*;
2. the tip of the sickle is higher than the handle.

Note Like all **AMULET(S)** and **TALISMAN(S)** of 'cold iron', the sickle should be an *old* one to give the greatest benefit.

SINGING

It's nice to sing . . . but when?

Sometimes it's dangerous

One often sings to express one's joy, but it is not always auspicious.

- *To sing whilst making bread* – is always unlucky.
- *To sing before breakfast* – will mean tears before night.
- *To sing whilst playing cards* – makes it certain you'll lose.

Our advice

Be careful where and when you sing. It is quite safe to sing while walking in the country.

SNEEZING

A sneeze – a sign from Heaven!

Omens from sneezing

If you sneeze, it is an omen, foretelling good or bad luck. So if you wish to know what the future has in store, observe carefully the circumstances in which you sneeze. The omens are good or bad depending on:

Which day of the week?

On MONDAY expect – danger.
On TUESDAY – a stranger.

On **WEDNESDAY** – a letter.
On **THURSDAY** – a present.
On **FRIDAY** – sorrow.
On **SATURDAY** – your lover.

What time of the day?

- Before breakfast – three sneezes mean a present.
- After a meal, especially dinner – a sneeze means good health.

How many times?

Once – a kiss.
Twice – a wish.
Three times – a letter.
Four times – a parcel.
Five times – silver.
Six times – gold.
Seven times – a secret.

In which direction?

- To the right – very *lucky*, especially at the start of a journey.
- To the left – very *unlucky*.

Important When anyone near you sneezes, always say 'God bless you'. It is *unlucky for you* to withhold this blessing.

SOCKS AND STOCKINGS

Good luck or a quarrel?

If you are a bit absent-minded!

- If you have put on one sock or stocking inside out, you can be certain that you will have a good day.
- If you have put on odd socks or stockings, this too is fortunate, especially if they are totally different colours or patterns.

Warning! Do not change your luck. In either of the above cases, you must leave your socks or stockings just as they are for the rest of the day: to correct your mistake would be to change your luck.

Ensure good luck

Always put on your left sock or stocking, or the left foot of your tights, before the right foot in the morning. That way you will have good luck all day.

Guard your health

Toothache: ladies, always put your left glove and stocking, or the left foot of your tights, on before your right and you will never have toothache.

Sore throat: tie your left sock or stocking, or the left leg of an old pair of tights, round your throat before going to bed at night and you'll be better by morning.

Choose the colour of your socks and stockings carefully

The colour of your socks or stockings influences your behaviour and the behaviour of anyone who sees them.

Black socks or stockings put the lower part of the body in harmony with the terrestrial element. They therefore favour all activities which are in harmony with the earth – and sexual activities in particular.

Grey or dark brown socks or stockings are in harmony with work, particularly hard and productive types of work: agriculture, crafts, etc.

Red, yellow, green or blue socks and stockings will help liven up anyone whose activities are not purely manual: these colours are also suitable for sporting activities and for leisure.

White socks or stockings are counter to the symbolism of the earth: to wear them is to suppress the instinctive forms of energy that come from the earth, and so detach oneself from the material world.

Our advice

Don't throw away dirty socks or stockings, even if they are very worn: it is wise to wash them before throwing them out. A sock or stocking becomes impregnated with sweat, which is charged at each step with your vital force. If you throw away your socks or stockings when they are thus impregnated, you are also throwing away your own vital force – and with it your power to take luck on the wing.

SPADE

The spade foretells death or a bad crop

The gardener's spade

If you are digging over the soil and the shaft of your spade breaks, gardening is not only going to be hard work, but the crop you grow will not be worth the labour put into it.

Avert this omen by putting back into the ground part of your last year's crop.

1. *Material required*

   a. The spade with the broken shaft, repaired and in usable condition.

   b. Some of the previous year's crop – this may take the form of dried, frozen or tinned goods, jelly, jam, or other preserves, but it *must* all have been grown in your own garden.

   c. A couple of tiles.

2. *Preparing the ground*

   a. Mark out in the centre of the garden a square whose sides are equal to four times the length of your footprint in the soil. *Note that the sides of the square must be parallel to the boundaries of the garden.*

   b. After marking out the square, dig it two spits deep (a spit is about a spade-length).

   c. In the centre of the hole you have made, dig a second hole, one spit deep, each side a spit in length. This hole must form a *diamond* within the larger hole.

   d. Place the produce from your garden at the bottom of this diamond-shaped hole and cover it with one or two tiles.

   e. Cover these with earth and fill up the surrounding hole.

Gardener, your spade has fallen down

If you have stuck your spade in the soil you have just been digging and it falls down, your crop will be less good than it was last year. *There is nothing you can do to avert this omen.*

The spade can be a malignant implement

- *Don't* carry your spade on your shoulder through the house. This is an invitation to disaster and means that a grave will soon be dug for one of the inhabitants (see also **AXE**).
- *Don't* wave a spade to attract someone's attention: his death is sure to follow.

Avert the omen, if someone waves a spade at *you*, by immediately picking up a handful of earth and throwing it towards (not at) him. This will avert the misfortune.

Our advice

You can make your spade less malignant by following two simple rules.

1. Always wipe the foot with mineral oil after cleaning it – never use animal or vegetable grease.
2. Keep the spade in an outbuilding – a garage, barn or shed – never in the house.

This way it will be reliable and safe.

SPIDER

Spider: a matter of timing

The spider is lucky or unlucky, according to the time of day you see it.

An evening spider is always lucky, in whatever circumstances you encounter it.

A morning spider is sometimes inauspicious.

Avert the omen by touching wood or 'cold iron', or spitting on the ground.

Spiders: bringers of wealth

- If a tiny money-spider runs over your clothes, it is a sign that you will be able to afford to replace them very soon. *Wind the spider round your head three times and the omen is even better.*
- If any sort of spider drops down on you from the ceiling, it is bringing you wealth, in particular a legacy.

The household spider: a lucky mascot

A spider may 'adopt' you and choose to live in your house, very often somewhere near the **HEARTH**.

If he does so, encourage him – let him be your mascot. He will not only kill the flies, but bring you happiness and prosperity.

When he comes out in the evening and walks around the floor, do not frighten him away. This is his house as well as yours! Above all:

Never kill a spider!

Under no circumstances whatsoever should you kill a spider. This will bring down on you the worst possible misfortune.

Don't forget the old saying:

> If you wish to live and thrive,
> Let a spider run alive.

SPITTING

When should you spit?

1. To attract luck

a. ***Spit for a good throw or aim***

Examples
On a tennis ball before serving.
On a baseball or cricket ball.
On a wood (at bowls).
On any object that has to be thrown accurately.
On an axe-blade before chopping wood.
On a cartridge before loading your gun.

b. ***Spit to summon up strength.***

Examples
A boxer spits on his gloves before a fight.
A woodcutter spits on his hands before getting down to work.

c. ***Spit to attract your catch***

Example
A fisherman spits in his net before putting it into the water, or on the hook before tying on the lure.

d. ***Spit to attract money***

Examples
A gambler spits under his chair before playing cards.
A market-trader spits on the first money he or she receives at the market that day.

2. To ward off evil

Spit:
- after a quarrel or any unpleasant incident;
- before going into a dangerous situation;
- to avert a bad omen, e.g. when you see a red-haired person or a single magpie;
- when you have been 'overlooked' by a person with the **EVIL EYE**.

3. To enhance a good omen

Increase your good luck by spitting when you see:

a white or piebald horse
a chimney sweep
the new moon (see **MOON**)

If you do so, you will double the luck that is already promised you by these omens.

SPITTLE

Spittle: know how to use it

By repeated licking or otherwise moistening with spittle, you can cure:

1. warts, corns and swellings;
2. the bite of reptiles and insects;
3. birthmarks (see **PREGNANCY**) and skin blemishes.

Important
To cure any of the above with spittle, the person who spits *must* be fasting.

Our advice

If you want to try any of these cures, set aside time for the treatment first thing every morning, before breakfast.

(See also **SPITTING**.)

STAIRS

The stairs: a dangerous place

Like **CROSSROADS** and other points of transition, the stairs are a dangerous place where you are exposed to evil influences.

Passing on the stairs

Passing anyone on the stairs, whoever it may be, is a very bad omen: it brings trouble within a few hours.

Avert the omen immediately by crossing your fingers as you pass (see **CROSSING THE FINGERS**).

Our advice

If you are at the head of the stairs and see someone coming up, wait until they have ascended. If you are at the foot, wait until they have come down. This way you will avoid misfortune.

Stumbling on the stairs

Going down – if you stumble going down the stairs, this is a very bad omen.

Going up – if you stumble going up, this is a sign of good fortune or else a wedding in the family.

STARS

The stars are beneficent

Seeing the first star of the evening appear in the sky brings good luck.

Starry nights are favourable

- To all who study at night.
- To amorous encounters.
- To harmonious evenings.
- To artistic creation.

Starless nights are ill-omened

They make for bad temper, lovers' tiffs, arguments in the course of the evening; they interfere with artistic creation.

Your horoscope will help you

We know the stars control the whole of biological and spiritual life. Your horoscope is therefore the source of countless presages which can help you to grasp at good luck when it comes your way. Unfortunately, good astrologers are hard to find.

Our advice: test your astrologer out

If you are having your horoscope cast, ask the astrologer to tell you first about your past and to pinpoint the years in which the important events of your life took place: first love, marriage, break-up, serious illnesses, surgery, birth of children, death of father, mother, brother or sister, divorce. The astrologer may make mistakes, omit certain events or add some which didn't occur. If in general he gets it all wrong, go to another astrologer. On the other hand, if he gives you certain detailed facts and the dates are correct, you can trust him.

Beware!

Don't wear jewellery representing your birth-sign.

Don't wear the metal or the stone or colour corresponding to your birth-sign in the hope that they will bring you luck. There is no foundation for the belief that wearing one's birth-sign (or the corresponding stone or colour) is always favourable.

Our advice: consult your astrologer

Your fate is not determined by your birth-sign alone. A horoscope is the synthesis of at least thirty-one different elements. It is only after a thorough study of these elements that a skilled astrologer can determine the stars and heavenly bodies which are favourable to you. To wear your birth-sign as jewellery obviously strengthens certain aspects of your personality; but the result of this may be good or bad for you, and this can only be discovered through a careful study of your horoscope.

STORK

The stork: bringer of luck

Storks foretell your good fortune

- If a pair of storks makes a nest on the roof of your house, they promise you a period of good luck.
- If the storks fly over your house, they are telling you of the coming birth of a child.

SWALLOW

The swallow: an augur of good or ill

Watch the swallows

- If they *make their nest* on your house, they will protect it from misfortune and bring it good luck.

145

- If they *desert their nest* before their annual migration abroad, they are warning you of misfortune to come.

Warning! Never disturb a swallow or destroy its nest, however inconvenient or messy: to do so will bring you bad luck.

TABLE

The dining-room table: don't misuse it

What not to do

Never put a pair of shoes or boots on the table – this is an omen of ill luck, and even death, for their owner (see under **SHOES**).

Never put a pair of bellows on the table, even purely ornamental ones – this is similarly ill-omened.

Beware thirteen!

Never invite thirteen people to dinner (make it twelve or fourteen). You would be sending one of your guests or yourself to an early death.

How to avert this ill omen

If against all expectations there are thirteen of you at table, lay a fourteenth place and serve food on to the extra place as if someone were there.

If someone knocks at the door during the meal, invite him (or her) to eat with you, as if the place were meant for him.

If no one appears during the meal, give the food served on the fourteenth plate to a neighbour or some needy person.

TALISMAN

Always wear your talisman: it will bring you luck

The power of the talisman

Unlike the **AMULET**, the talisman's function is not to protect but:

146

1. to help you acquire luck or healing powers;
2. to bring you success in work and love.

A personal treasure

Your talisman may be a unique object: something special to you, your family or even your nation – like the Stone of Scone.

A particular piece of family jewellery may likewise act as a talisman (see, for example, **CAMEO**).

Or you may have a personal 'mascot' – a cuddly toy, for example – which seems to bring you luck whenever it is with you.

Other powerful talismans

- Coins with holes through them, such as the old French sou (see **COIN**).
- Adder stones,* i.e. small stones with holes through them.

Note The coins must have been minted with holes, and the adder stones got theirs naturally by weathering. Don't try to 'make' such talismans: YOU CANNOT MANUFACTURE LUCK.

Ought you to wear your birth sign?

Wearing one's birth sign is not always positive. Before deciding if you can or should wear it as a talisman, have your horoscope cast by a good astrologer: only he can advise you.

Our secret

Create a bond between you and your talisman. If you have just acquired one, wear it for the first time on the morning of the third day after the first quarter of the moon as shown by the ☽ sign on your calendar or in your diary.

Example: ☽ TUESDAY
WEDNESDAY
THURSDAY: wear the talisman for the first time.

On this first day, put the talisman under your pillow at night, before going to sleep: put it on again the following morning as soon as you wake up. You should sleep for *seven consecutive nights* with your talisman under your pillow and wear it for *seven days* before it really works for you.

---

* So-called because they were believed to be formed from the saliva of snakes.   Ed.

147

TEA

Tea: a prophetic drink

Making tea: attend to the omens

- If you accidentally leave the lid off the pot – a stranger is coming.
- If two women pour from the same pot – before the year is out one of them, or some member of her family, will have a baby.

Warning! Never stir the tea in the pot: this will cause quarrels.

Reading the tea-leaves

Reading the future from tea-leaves at the bottom of a cup is complicated and best left to a professional or good amateur fortune-teller. However, you may easily read the omens from the stalks which float on the top of tea.

Reading the stalks

A *single stalk* – a stranger is coming.
A *hard, woody stalk* – the stranger will be a man.
A *soft stalk* – it will be a woman.

To find out when he or she will arrive

1. Put the stalk on the back of your left hand.
2. Strike or nudge your left hand with your right until the stalk falls off. As many blows are needed to dislodge it, so many days will pass before the visitor arrives.

THEATRE

Theatre people: some signs of fate

Signs that tell you the show will be a flop

- If the 'tag' or last line of the play is spoken before the first night.
- If the dress rehearsal was perfect.

Our advice to all companies

Adopt a stray cat, look after it, and make it the show's mascot. It will bring you luck, provided that you:

a) never kick it;
b) never let it run across the stage.

Both these things are unlucky.

Before the show

Don't look at the audience through the curtain from the side of the stage: this is *very unlucky*.

Our advice

If you want to see the audience, look through the little hole that is made in the centre of the curtain for this purpose.

In the theatre

Don't wear anything yellow – this would be very unlucky.
Don't say the words 'rope', 'string', 'bad luck', 'good luck', 'success' or 'flop'.
Don't whistle in a dressing-room: this means that one of the cast will be dismissed.

Avert the omen by making whoever has whistled go outside and turn round three times.

On the set

Don't have real mirrors on the set (see **MIRROR**).

Your first entrance

Your first entrance is very important.

- If your shoes squeak, you will be a success.
- If you stumble as you go on, you will forget your lines.
- If your clothes catch on the scenery, you will be a failure.

Avert the omen, if possible, by going back and beginning again.

THIRTEEN

Thirteen: all or nothing

According to your personality, the number thirteen is either entirely lucky or entirely unlucky, as far as you are concerned.

- If the number thirteen brings you good luck, earmark any Friday 13 for new undertakings.
- If the number thirteen brings you bad luck, don't start anything on Friday 13.

A special case

Being *thirteen at table brings bad luck* whatever the circumstances (see **TABLE**).

UMBILICAL CORD

The umbilical cord: protects your child

Use it as a charm

When your baby is born, it is very unusual for the hospital to suggest giving you the umbilical cord. As a rule, it is frozen and sold to a pharmaceutical or cosmetic laboratory. But ask for it: they will give it to you, as it's yours. (Get them to put it in a jar containing some alcohol.)

Making the charm

Wait until your husband comes to visit you and ask him to cut 2 cm off the umbilical cord and put it somewhere to dry (e.g. near a radiator).

When it's dry, put it in a little white silk sachet and hang it round your child's neck.

This lucky charm has the power to protect your baby from ill-fortune and to improve the growth of his bones.

150

Our advice

As soon as you leave the hospital, go and bury the rest of the umbilical cord at the foot of a young tree (preferably an oak). In this way, you guarantee a lifetime of good health for your child.

UMBRELLA

Umbrella: take great care

Things to remember not to do

Don't open your umbrella indoors: this would bring you bad luck and aggravate every bad omen.

Don't go out with your umbrella when the sun is shining: you might attract the rain.

Don't lay an umbrella on a bed: this is very unlucky.

Don't give an umbrella as a gift: misfortune will go with it.

If you drop your umbrella

If you drop your umbrella, don't pick it up: this is a very bad omen. If it falls, allow someone else to pick it up for you.

Our advice

Treat your umbrella with great care and think of it as a friend.

UNDERWEAR

Your underwear: try putting it on back to front to change your luck

If your day has started badly, lock your door, take off your underwear and put it on again back to front: this will change the course of events.

Our advice: all the winners next to your skin

Look at the section of 'favourable colours' under **COLOURS** and make sure you don't disturb their harmony.

Coloured underwear should be matched with the other clothes you have on, to increase the potential of good luck already acquired by wearing them.

VERVAIN

Vervain: an all-purpose herb

As an aphrodisiac

Vervain has long been used in love-philtres to rekindle a dying love.

Men: put three seeds of vervain in a white linen bag and hang it round your neck. (Vervain seeds may be bought from seed-merchants, especially those specializing in herbs.)

To protect your house against malign influences

If hung on the door, a spray of vervain will prevent the entry into your house of all malign influences.

To guard against 'overlooking'

If you think that something belonging to you has been 'overlooked', whether deliberately or inadvertently (see **EVIL EYE**), rub it with a few leaves of vervain.

Example: if you are a sportsman who persistently misses his aim, try rubbing the barrel of your gun with vervain. It may have been overlooked. (This won't of course help if your only problem is that you're a bad shot!)

To prevent nightmares

Háng a necklace of the dried roots of vervain around your neck when you go to bed – you will have no bad dreams.

As a cure for insomnia

Using 1 teaspoonful of dried vervain* to each cup, add to boiling water and allow to steep for 3–5 minutes. Strain and drink (not more than three cups daily).

Our advice: to ensure a harmonious evening

Follow a Roman custom and steep some leaves of vervain in water overnight. Next day, sprinkle this water in the room in which you will be entertaining your guests. You will find each other's company all the more pleasant.

WASHING

Washing: a dangerous business

Every time you wash yourself, a little of your life-essence as well as dirt passes into the water. This leaves you temporarily exposed to mischance and misfortune. So,

Take care! Follow the rules

1. Don't wash your hands in the same water as someone else – or you will quarrel before nightfall.

Exception If you have known each other intimately for seven years or more, you are free to break this rule – it does not affect you.

Correct procedure Other than this, you may share the same water with someone else only if you make the sign of the cross on the water with your forefinger or spit in it before washing. These actions avert the bad luck (see **CROSS** and **SPITTING**).

---

* Be careful what you buy as vervain. The French commonly use the name 'verveine' and the English 'verbena' for both vervain itself (*Verbena officinalis*) and Lemon verbena (*Lippia citriodora*), and this has caused much confusion. Lemon verbena is often used as a tisane, and can be bought in the form of teabags from health-food stores and chemists. It makes a refreshing drink and is mildly sedative, but it is *not* the 'Holy Herb' of the ancients and does not share vervain's magical properties. So study the packet carefully. It is probably simpler to grow your own or gather it from the wild (it grows in Britain, Europe and North America). Harvest the side shoots (both leaves and flowering tips) before the flowers are fully open in June.   Ed.

2. Don't pass the soap to another person – this also brings bad luck, especially if you are sisters.

Correct procedure If you are forced to share a bar of soap, don't pass it from hand to hand. One of you must put it down for the other to take up.

Don't wash away luck

Mothers – don't wash a child's right hand until he is one year old or he will never gather riches. Use a damp flannel to wipe it instead.

Fishermen – if the fishing is exceptionally good, don't wash. Wait till the trip is ended or you may lose your luck.

Miners – be careful how often you wash your back. You may be inviting roof-falls.

WATER

Dreaming of water foretells some misfortune

If you dream of standing water

Ponds and pools foretell stagnation in your present situation, so save your energy for later: it's not the moment to start anything.

If you dream of cascades or waterfalls

You are temporarily under a spell: your current projects will founder.

If you dream of a river or a stream

Your current hopes will not be realized, although apparently all set for success.

Warning! If you dream that you are drowning, this is a portent of death.

Our advice

When you have dreamt of water, take a cold or lukewarm bath the morning after, with some salt added. This will partially ward off the bad omen.

WEDDING

Study the omens: your future depends on it

Get married on a favourable day

As a rule, every day of the week is favourable to marriage, except Friday. As regards months, consider the following dates when fixing the date of your wedding.

January
Favourable dates: 2, 4, 11, 19 and 21

February
1, 3, 10, 19 and 21

March
3, 5, 13, 20 and 23

April
2, 4, 12, 20 and 22

May
One should never get married in May. However, if it's unavoidable, these are the least ill-omened dates of the month: 2, 4, 12 and 23. *The worst day in the year for anyone to get married is Friday 13 May.*

June
The most favourable month for marriage. The most auspicious dates are: 1, 3, 11 and 21

July
1, 3, 12, 19, 21 and 31

August
2, 11, 18, 20 and 30

September
1, 9, 16, 18 and 28

October
1, 8, 15, 17 and 29

November
5, 11, 13, 22 and 25

December
1, 8, 10, 23 and 29.

Be careful

From these dates, choose one:

- which doesn't fall on a Friday;
- which doesn't fall between the full moon and the new moon;
- which isn't your birthday – or your future spouse's birthday,

unless you were both born on the same day (the year doesn't matter), in which case choose that date in preference to any other.

The days of the week

They are also very important. Bear in mind when making your choice the sort of future you wish your relationship to embody.

> Monday for wealth,
> Tuesday for health,
> Wednesday the best day of all.
> Thursday for losses,
> Friday for crosses,
> And Saturday for no luck at all.

Our advice

If Saturday must be your choice for purely practical reasons, remember that:

1. it is less positively inauspicious than Friday;
2. the effects of the omen can be neutralized by making sure that everything else is just right.

The time of day

Don't forget that a wedding *should always take place before sundown*.

The weather is important too!

The weather on your wedding-day foretells the future of your marriage.

'Happy is the bride that the sun shines on' – if it's fine for the time of year, your marriage will be a happy one.

It is very lucky, too, for the bride to see a rainbow on her way to the church.

Other auspicious omens

It is extremely lucky if the bride or any other member of the wedding party:

- meets a black cat on the way to church;
- meets a sweep, especially if he offers his congratulations and walks a little way beside the procession.

Inauspicious omens

It is extremely unlucky:

- for a bride on her way to the church to meet, or even catch sight of, a funeral;
- for a pig to cross the road in front of the wedding party;
- for the bride's car to fail to start;
- for the wedding party to enter the churchyard through the lych-gate or the north door of the church.

Avert the omen in all these cases by crossing your fingers (middle finger over forefinger).

Dropping the ring

Dropping the ring before or during the wedding ceremony is a very bad omen.

If the bridegroom drops it, it means that he will be the first to die; if the bride, vice versa.

If it comes to rest on a memorial stone on the floor, it foretells (if the gravestone is a woman's) early death for the bride, (if a man's) an early death for the groom.

Our advice

Hold firmly on to the ring and do not fumble. In this case, as in everything else:

Make your own luck

Brides and grooms: it is unlucky for you to see each other on your wedding morning before you meet at church – so make certain you do not do so.

Grooms: on your wedding-day, put three grains of coarse salt in the left-hand pocket of your jacket: this will ensure good luck.

The wedding-dress

'Something old, something new'

Brides, to symbolize your new state of life, every item you wear on your wedding-day should be new, except:

'something old'
'something borrowed' } try to kill two birds with one stone by borrowing your mother's, or some other family member's, wedding veil

'something blue' – a ribbon, perhaps, on your underwear (it need not be visible)

Never wear

black or purple – which signify mourning;
green – which signifies that mourning will soon be worn;
yellow – which signifies 'forsworn';
brown – which signifies that your husband will never rise to fortune.

Do wear (in this order):

white or silver;
blue, pink or gold;
grey or fawn.

It is unlucky

- To make your own wedding-dress.
- To put on your complete wedding-dress before the day.
- To see yourself in your complete wedding-dress in a mirror before the ceremony. (See **MIRROR**.)
- To try on the complete wedding-dress at once.
- To finish the complete wedding-dress before the day.

Our advice

When you are being fitted for your wedding-dress, try it on in separate sections.

Ask for a short length of hem to be left unsewn until the very last moment.

Do not look in the mirror until you are on the point of leaving for the wedding – and then leave off some small item such as your shoes or gloves.

The wedding-cake

The wedding-cake is a symbol of fertility and abundance.

Brides

You must cut the first slice of your wedding-cake, or your marriage will be childless. (Your husband may help, by laying his hand over yours.)

You must keep a slice yourself, until the christening of your first child: then your husband will be faithful.

Wedding guests

Do accept and *eat* a piece of the wedding-cake. To refuse would bring bad luck to the young couple and to yourself.

Do throw some rice, not on to the young couple, but around them as they come out of the church or Registry Office: this will ensure their prosperity.

Do, as they leave for their honeymoon, fire a few shots into the air or let off some fireworks, to drive away ill fortune.

WEDDING RING

The wedding ring: a source of omens

Your wedding ring is a source of omens throughout your married life.

Your wedding ring turns black or cracks: danger!

Your wedding ring can tell you how your spouse is getting on when one of you is away. Silver wedding rings are particularly good for this purpose.

If your silver wedding ring suddenly turns black, this means that your husband or wife needs to contact you at the earliest possible moment.

Gold rings also sometimes crack for no apparent reason.

These incidents are rare and no one can give an explanation. They always indicate *a serious situation of an urgent nature*. Your partner may be seriously ill or may perhaps need some document you hold or may even need your help in some sort of family problem. Anything is possible. (See also **KNIFE**.)

Our advice

Get in touch with your spouse immediately.

Taking off, losing or breaking your wedding ring

Ladies, don't do it!

A. To take off your wedding ring, or to have it fall off, before the birth of your first child is very unlucky.

Avert the omen by having your husband replace the ring at once.

B. If you lose your wedding ring, it is a sign of coming misfortune.

Avert the omen by getting your husband to replace the ring with another as soon as possible.

C. If your wedding ring breaks, this is the worst omen of all: it means the ending of the marriage, possibly by death.

Avert the omen by very quickly replacing the ring.

WHISTLING

Whistling can be dangerous

Be careful where you whistle

Like **SINGING**, whistling is an expression of joy that under certain circumstances can be extremely ill-omened. Be careful where you whistle.

- To whistle down a mine – may bring about a disaster.
- To whistle in a **THEATRE**, especially the dressing-rooms – is a sign that someone (not always the whistler) will soon be out of work.
- To whistle on a **SHIP** – whistles up a wind. This is doubly unlucky if the whistler is a woman.

Warning! A whistling woman is as unlucky on land as she is at sea: she brings misfortune on others, sometimes even death.

Our advice

Ladies – never whistle. It can do no good.

Whistling after dark

This is a most ill-advised action whether indoors or without. It may summon all manner of malignant entities.

Negate the summons If someone ill-advisedly whistles after dark in your home, send him or her outside immediately, to walk three times round the house. This will cancel the summons that has been given.

WISHBONE

Wishbone: eat a chicken and make a wish

If you have been given the part of the chicken which includes the wishbone and have eaten the meat around it, follow this procedure.

A. Take one of the ends of the wishbone and offer the other to the person sitting next to you.
B. Both hold the wishbone by crooking your little finger round it.
C. Now pull together on the ends of the wishbone while each of you makes a wish.

The one who breaks off the larger part of the bone will have the wish fulfilled.

Warning!
1. You must neither speak nor laugh during these proceedings.
2. You must tell no one what your wish was until after it has been fulfilled.

WOOD

Touch wood and avert an omen

What sort of wood?

In an emergency any sort of wood will do, but the best is oak or, failing that, apple, ash, hawthorn, hazel or willow. These are sacred trees which have the power to protect you.

In what circumstances?

- When you have encountered anything ill-omened.
- When a taboo has been broken, e.g. by the speaking of a forbidden word (see for examples under **SHIP**).

Suit the action to the words

It is not enough simply to say 'touch wood' – you *must* suit the action to the words for it to be effective.

To touch your head, signifying wooden-headedness, is of course a joke: it has no protective value.

Our advice

Keep a small piece of wood from one of the 'sacred' trees in your pocket or bag: then you will be ready.

Important All omens which can be averted by touching wood, can equally well be rendered ineffective by touching 'cold iron'.